KINGDOM TRANSFORMATION

Discover God's incredible life in a suffering world

REVISED EDITION

Kevin Michalek

World rights reserved. This book or any portion thereof may not be copied or reproduced in any form or manner whatever, except as provided by law, without the written permission of the publisher, except by a reviewer who may quote brief passages in a review.

The author assumes full responsibility for the accuracy of all facts and quotations as cited in this book. The opinions expressed in this book are the author's personal views and interpretations, and do not necessarily reflect those of the publisher.

This book is provided with the understanding that the publisher is not engaged in giving spiritual, legal, medical, or other professional advice. If authoritative advice is needed, the reader should seek the counsel of a competent professional.

Copyright © 2017 Kevin Michalek
Copyright © 2017, 2022 TEACH Services, Inc.
ISBN-13: 978-1-4796-0738-9 (Paperback)
ISBN-13: 978-1-4796-0739-6 (ePub)
ISBN-13: 978-1-4796-0740-2 (Mobi)
Library of Congress Control Number: 2017905751

Cover design and layout by Shana Michalek

Published by

This book is dedicated to:

Greg Boyd,
whose gospel kingdom concepts inspired this book
and made me process the gospel
in a more experiential and pragmatic way.

Bill Liversidge,
who was a master of the inductive method
and made me understand the gospel in clear lines
through the life, death, and resurrection of Christ.

My family,
who gave me the time and, through their sacrifice,
encouragement to carry it forward.

"It is refreshing to see in Kevin's book Christ centeredness and the greatest foundation of Christian living - Christ in you."
—Grant Agadjanian, President, Creative Media Ministries, Assoc. Director and speaker at Sure Harvest Ministries

"In his book, Kingdom Transformation, Kevin provides a basis for what kingdom living really is... The living Christ in us! This book not only challenges us as Christians but also provides some thought provoking questions at the end of each chapter making it ideal for group study"
—Karen Lewis, Pastor with Minn. Conf. of Seventh Day-Adventists and author of *Lifting up Jesus Bible Studies*

Table of Contents

Introduction 7
Abbreviations 10
   1. The Kingdom's Love Covenant Gospel 11
   2. Kingdom of Adoption 19
   3. Kingdom of Holiness 29
   4. A Kingdom of Priests 37
   5. Kingdom Awareness 49
   6. Kingdom Fearlessness 56
   7. The Single-minded Kingdom 65
   8. The Kingdom of Abounding Grace 73
   9. God's Kingdom Picture 83
   10. Kingdom Centeredness 93
   11. The Counter Kingdom 100
   12. The Difference Between the Two Kingdoms 106
   13. The King's Kingdom 116
   14. The Discerning Kingdom 122
   15. Kingdom Unity 130
   16. Maturing into the Kingdom 138
   17. Kingdom Indwelled Transformation 144
Bibliography 148

Introduction

Defining the Kingdom

What exactly is the kingdom? We hear a lot about it, but still have little idea of what it entails, how everyone is affected by it, where it is, why it is, who's involved and in which kingdom they are involved. Let's start with the word "kingdom." The Greek word is *basileiva* (bas-il-i'-ah). It represents the king's dominion. The Old English usage of the word is derived from "king" and "dom." The word "dom" had several usages in Old English; one was related to "doom" or "judge." A judge or "deemster" was to deem (judge) or pronounce one's doom. Therefore, we can say that the king judges. However, the word "dome" is also related to "dom" or "doom," and the Latin *domus/duomo* means is "covering, roof, or canopy"[1] That is why domed cathedrals were called basilicas in the first few centuries of Hellenistic church culture. The domed church Hagia Sophia in Istanbul is a perfect example of a basilica church. Therefore, the English word equivalent is composed of the house or covering of the king. However, there are two kingdoms—the one that Jesus rules[2] and one that Satan rules, which encompasses all the kingdoms of this earth.[3]

Therefore, we have two kingdoms that are competing for every human

---

1. C.T. Onions, *The Oxford Dictionary of English Etymology* (Oxford: Oxford University Press, 1966), 283.
2. See John 18:36 and Luke 17:20, 21.
3. See 1 John 5:19 and Revelation 17:18; 18:3.

that has ever lived, is living, and ever will live. Sometimes Satan's kingdom seems harmless as he clothes it with religiosity, love, and compassion, but underneath these cloaks, he is a stealthy mastermind trying to gather all of his followers under his domain with tools such as manipulation, deception, and force. Jesus' kingdom is contrastingly marked by peace, joy, patience, and other fruits of the Spirit that all stem from His love.

John Yoder wrote, *"the cross is not a detour or a hurdle on the way to the kingdom, nor is it even the way to the kingdom; it is the kingdom come."*[4] The cross defines that God is love. And John says that we can know that God is love because He gave us His Life. And His life is the Kingdom.[5] In our world, many try to find happiness in many ways, but we will fall under one of these two kingdoms. Even by default, if we don't decide, we've decided under which kingdom we are falling, and many times unaware. We will look at what Jesus says about the kingdom and how Satan desires to misguide and manipulate his concepts of Scripture to think we may be with God when in actuality we may be falling under his domain.

The primary purpose of this book is to allow God to dwell within us and look at the practical aspects of how He works in us so that we recognize that we are under His domain. We will see that there are many different words and concepts in Scripture that have the same or similar definitions of what the kingdom is.

Living under the king-dome is the same idea as dwelling in God's sanctuary. This is clearly brought forth in Psalm 27, where it states, *"One thing have I desired of the LORD, that will I seek after; that I may dwell in the house of the LORD all the days of my life, to behold the beauty of the LORD, and to inquire in his temple. For in the time of trouble he shall hide me in his pavilion: in the secret of his tabernacle shall he hide me; he shall set me up upon a rock. And now shall mine head be lifted up above mine enemies round about me: therefore, will I offer in his tabernacle sacrifices of joy; I will sing, yea, I will sing praises unto the LORD."*[6] We can clearly see that David found refuge within God's sanctuary and he desired to continually seek God and dwell with Him all of his life. Furthermore, David states that when he dwells there, he is raised to a higher plane above his enemies, and because of these aspects of his union with God, he offered sacrifices of praise and thanksgiving.

David's experience is one of peace amidst trial, beholding God's beauty, and finding safety in the Tabernacle, and because of these, he

---

4. John Yoder, *The Politics of Jesus* (Grand Rapids, MI: Wm. B. Eerdmans Publishing, 1994), 61.
5. 1 John 3:16.
6. Psalm 27:4, 6.

puts forth praise to his King. The first verse in the Bible on the sanctuary describes God desiring to be among His people.[7] God has always desired to indwell Himself within His people and be among them as well. In Exodus 25:8 God says, *"let them make me a sanctuary that I may dwell among them."* If we replace the phrase "among them" to "within them" then we have the same concept as the kingdom concept. Let it be for all of us that being under the dome of the King is where we desire to be and where God desires to have us. For Jesus, the mutual indwelling of Himself within His people allows for a very intimate and rewarding experience.

We'll also look at how certain Greek words have a profound impact upon how and what Jesus, Paul, and other New Testament writers said. It was their intention that the meaning of these words, which poured forth into the early church, culminate into a dynamic and active body of believers in Christ.

We will also examine what Jesus intended the kingdom to be. I want to thank Greg Boyd for a series of sermons that catapulted the kingdom concept in this book. The kingdom, which is dynamic and living, as Jesus is, never compartmentalizes faith, as Jesus never did; the kingdom ascribes unconditional and unsurpassable worth, as Jesus did; and the kingdom stifles judgment and assessment of others, as Jesus did. Kingdom people look like Jesus because the King lives in those who are under His dome. Furthermore, Paul describes in Colossians[8] that we have moved from the kingdom or power of darkness to God's Kingdom. Another way to put it is that we have been transplanted from Satan's domain to God's domain. We will also learn how some of the aspects of the kingdom formulate a beautiful picture of God and how we can participate in that picture.

The fact remains that Jesus always desired to incarnate Himself in his people. The fullness of Christ is offered to all who desire Christ to live in them. As all have already benefited from his death, His life is what He yearns to give us.[9] The beauty of Christ is in the reality that we can share with God's purpose and align ourselves with His will to put His glorious riches on display, and those riches are based upon His love. There is no higher experience and biblical directive than for God to indwell Himself within His people. *"The Kingdom of God is built through one simple method: the King reveals his course of action, and we subject ourselves to his will by cooperating with his revelation to reveal his glory."*[10]

---

7. Exodus 25:8 is the first verse in Scripture on the sanctuary.
8. See Colossians 1:13.
9. See 2 Corinthians 5:21.
10. Jeff Christopherson, *The Kingdom Matrix* (Boise, ID: Russell Media, 2012), 34.

Abbreviations

KJV: *King James version,* known in Britain as the *Authorized Version* (1611; Revised 1769; based on the TR).

ISV: *The Holy bible: International Standard Version, ISV Foundation* (1996-2012).

NASB: *New American Standard Bible, Lockman Foundation* (1960, 1962, 1963, 1968, 1971, 1972, 1973, 1975, 1977; *Updated Edition* 1995)

NET: *The NET Bible/New English Translation, Biblical Studies Press* (2005).

WEB: Michael Paul Johnson, *World English Bible* (1997).

EMTV: *English Majority Text Version: New Testament,* trans. Paul W. Esposito (209).

ESV: *The English Standard Version*, Crossway Bibles (2001).

NHEB: Wayne A. Mitchell, *New Heart English Bible* (2008).

AKJV: Michael Peter (Stone) Engelbrite, *American King James Version* (1999).

BBE: S. H. Hooke, *Bible in Basic English* (1949).

The Kingdom's Love Covenant Gospel

The Foundation for the New Life in Christ

As we begin this journey to understand the kingdom, we first want to set the foundation for what Christ the Messiah accomplished for all mankind and then reveal the deeper purposes of His work for all the universe.

Christ came on the scene in first-century Palestine at the appointed time.[11] The Jews were looking for a warrior-king to relieve them of Roman oppression. However, the function and role of Jesus Christ was totally misunderstood by some and intentionally not desired by others. Therefore, we will look at two aspects of Jesus's role as the Messiah— what Jesus was meant to be and how God's gospel of Christ was based on a covenant of love.

The Crisis of the Christ

The Greek word *christos*, from which "Christ" is derived, simply means "anointed one." The Hebrew equivalent gave us the English word "messiah." Therefore, if Jesus is the anointed one, then for what was Jesus anointed? When Jesus came to His hometown of Nazareth after His baptism, He was appointed to read from the book of Isaiah, in chapter sixty one. Luke's version of the story in chapter 4 verse 18 states, *"The Spirit of the Lord is upon me, because He has anointed me to proclaim good news*

---

11. Galatians 4:4.

to the poor. He sent me to heal the broken hearted, to proclaim release to the captives, recovering of sight to the blind, to deliver those that are crushed."[12] Therefore, Jesus was anointed specifically for 1) proclaiming good news to the poor, 2) healing the brokenhearted, 3) proclaiming release to the captives, 4) regaining the sight to those who are blind, and 5) setting those free who are oppressed. If we look at each of these descriptions or duties of Christ, we can see that not only do they convey actual physical healings, but they have spiritual applications as well. Proclaiming good news can be to the spiritually poor as well as to the physically poor. Receiving spiritual sight is at least as important as receiving physical sight. The same can be said about being released from the captivity of sin. As a matter of fact, the spiritual implications go beyond any physical realities.

Therefore, the degree to which I allow Christ to heal me spiritually is the degree to which I become a partaker of His divine nature. True healing comes from allowing Christ in me. However, many of us are self-deceived, thinking that we don't even need spiritual healing in our lives, or that we are spiritually healed when in fact we may not be. What is interesting is what John says to those who deny this healing. John says, *"You have an anointing from the Holy One, and you all have knowledge. I have not written to you because you don't know the truth, but because you know it, and because no lie is of the truth. Who is the liar but he who denies that Jesus is the Christ. This is the Antichrist, he who denies the Father and the Son. Whoever denies the Son doesn't have the Father. He who confesses the Son has the Father also."*[13]

First, John mentions that believers have been anointed from the Holy One, which is Christ. Second, whoever denies that Jesus is the Christ is an antichrist and a liar, and no lie is of the truth. Therefore, if we deny what Jesus was anointed to do, which was heal the brokenhearted, give sight to the blind, and set the captives free from sin and oppression, then we deny that Jesus is the Christ. It's a denial of the gospel itself. A lot of people believe Jesus is the Savior, but not all of them believe He is the anointed One. Many of them refuse to be spiritually healed and receive spiritual sight. To many Christians, the sins of this world are too appealing, so they refuse the gospel of freedom and restoration. In other words, many profess Jesus, but they don't want to be changed by Him. It's unbelief in what Christ can do, and while many refuse the change, they also lack the conviction of the good news. It's easy to pin the antichrist to a system, but

---

12. NHEB
13. 1 John 2:20-23, WEB.

what John is telling us is that a denial of what Jesus desires to do in restoring our lives is refusing the Christ, thereby making us an individual antichrist. Therefore, an antichrist is one who is in denial of what Jesus, the Anointed One, is to do. Victory and overcoming have become an illusion to many, and this is the spirit of antichrist. Many think *It doesn't matter what I do. Christ loves me no matter what my condition is.* However, He doesn't leave us where He finds us. Preaching true deliverance is the healing of the gospel message. It was for this freedom that Christ set us free.[14]

All who desire the new life of Christ and allow Him to dwell inside them are the legitimate citizens of His kingdom. The daily struggle of faith is to put our fallen nature out of the way and allow Christ to do what He desires to do. When we allow Christ to indwell Himself in us, His attitude toward sin becomes our attitude toward sin. It will be Jesus in you who will not have the desire for sin. It's not trying to fight a spiritual warfare with a little help from Jesus; rather, it's allowing the "fullness of God" to dwell within us.[15] This is the promise—that the true tabernacle would be with and in men.[16] It's not us, but rather Christ in us, that wins the victory. It's Christ in us that makes us victorious. Even in 1 John 4:15 John says that when "God abides in the one who acknowledges that Jesus is the Son of God, and he abides in God." (ISV). There is a mutually indwelling based upon acknowledging Jesus, or as some versions say confessing Jesus, as the Son of God, sent to be the saviour of the world. Also, 1 John 2:20 states that we have been anointed to bring this good news to others, and 1 Peter 2:9 states that the reason that we have become a priesthood is to "declare the excellence of God, who called us out of darkness into His marvelous light." In other words, my life becomes a testimony of Jesus a testimony working in me, and then Christ in me reaches others to bring the anointed message of Isaiah to others. How essential it is, then, to develop the daily habit of allowing God to indwell Himself in you. Let's now look at how the everlasting kingdom covenant of God, based on God's motivating love, makes this happen.

> *All who desire the new life of Christ and allow Him to dwell inside them are the legitimate citizens of His kingdom.*

---

14. Galatians 5:1, NET
15. Ephesians 3:19.
16. See Exodus 25:8; Revelation 21:3.

The Crisis of Covenant Love

Looking beyond our limited understanding of what the kingdom is, we will see that there are several representations for what the kingdom of God is represented as. As we explore the kingdom theme, we will understand how these different definitions relate to each other.

In other words, it's like a domino effect. Once we see deeper meanings of what the kingdom is, we can then see a chain of verses that form and connect to each other, further defining the kingdom. As we just saw the foundationally good news of the kingdom through the Christ in this chapter, we will further explore God's covenant as it relates to the gospel and look at how God defines His everlasting covenant with humanity.

The Jewish word for *"covenant"* is *bariyth* (ber-eeth) *or b'rit*. The Greek equivalent is *diatheke*. Though the word may be used for many covenants in the Old Testament, it ultimately signifies a mutual commitment based on love between two parties. Therefore, God's covenant with mankind is one of love. As in the Hebrew, a "chesed" steadfast love is the distinctive quality of the covenant relationship; it's a quality of God as defined in Psalms and Jeremiah[17] and it's also a "required quality of God's covenant partners."[18] God's covenant is also linked to His kingdom, as in Luke 22:29 where it states that "God has *'appointed'* (*Diatheke* = covenant) *you a kingdom...*" Therefore, God's covenant, which is based upon love, is extensively linked to God's kingdom. The idea of the New Covenant is connected to the life, death, and resurrection of Jesus, as well as the Lord's supper.[19] It was on the basis of God's love to and for us that Jesus bore the cross and allowed us the opportunity to become part of His kingdom so that His love could be incorporated into mankind. However, as we just saw, it's us allowing the anointed One, the Christ, to implement His life into us.

As in the Old Testament, the New Testament word for "righteousness" is closely related to the word "covenant" (*dikaiosune*), and God's righteousness is revealed in His character of love. Therefore, to be a partaker of God's covenant is to be a partaker of His love and righteousness. When we set up habits in our lives that partake of Christ and enter His life through this mutually indwelling, two things happen. One, we have given God the permission to fully cleanse, restore, and heal us, thereby

---

17. See Psalm 136 and Jeremiah 9:24.
18. W. VanGemeren, *New International Dictionary of O.T. Theology and Exegesis* (Grand Rapids, MI: Zondervan Publishing, 1997), vol. 1, 752. Also see Psalms 50:5.
19. See Matthew 26:28; Mark 14:24; Luke 22:20.

partaking of all the qualities and characteristics of Christ Himself, and two, we are anointed to share this new life with others. Even God's goodness shines through in our repentance, because in the end, entering God's covenant kingdom through faith is possible only because of His goodness, which leads us to repentance.[20] Therefore, it's because of God's goodness that this process begins.

The heart of the New Covenant is that God desires to be "with us" or "within us."[21] Jesus even said that God's kingdom is "within," and to the degree that we allow this He writes His love Covenant on our hearts.[22] God put forth the idea of His love covenant at Mt. Sinai. Israel was to be God's special people, and He would bear them up on eagle's wings and bring them to Himself.[23] God's purpose has always been to make a people for His possession.[24] He has waited a long time to have an intimate indwelling with His people, as Zechariah described that experience when He says, "in that day" I will dwell in the midst of thee."[25]

O. Palmer Robertson brings to our attention the fact that this indwelling is a progressive theme in Scripture. "It moves from the figure of the Tabernacle to the figure of the Temple to the city of God. It involves the incarnate Christ, the church of Christ, and the final glorification of God's people. The essence of the covenantal relation found its initial fulfillment in the form of the tabernacle." [26] Also, Exodus 25:8 describes that one of the major purposes of the tabernacle was so that God could indwell Himself with His people. Ezekiel also adds, "Moreover I will make a covenant of peace with them; it shall be an everlasting covenant with them: and I will place them, and multiply them, and will set my sanctuary in the midst of them for evermore. My tabernacle also shall be with them: yea, I will be their God, and they shall be my people. **And the heathen shall know that I the LORD do sanctify Israel, when my sanctuary shall be in the midst of them for evermore.**"[27] Therefore, we can see that God desired to be among and within them to sanctify them or separate them for a holy purpose,

---

20. Romans 2:4.
21. Exodus 25:8; Matthew 1:23.
22. See Luke 17:21.
23. See Exodus 19:4, 5.
24. See Exodus, 19:5; Deuteronomy 4:20.
25. Zechariah 2:11. Some versions have the word "midst" in Luke 17:21 referring to Jesus as the kingdom within their midst. Other versions reference Jesus in Luke 17:21 as "among" you, thereby referencing Jesus is the kingdom whether in the midst or among us.
26. O. Palmer Robertson, *The Christ of the Covenants* (Phillipsburg, NJ: Presbyterian and Reformed Publishing, 1980), 49.
27. Ezekiel 37:26-28.

which was to put God on display, within His people, before the nations.

Robertson further states, "In terms of the consummate experience of the new covenant, the theme of Immanuel as the sum of the covenant also plays a central role. God 'tabernacles' in human flesh by the presence of the incarnate Son. God's people are the temple of the Lord, "being built together into a dwelling of God in the Spirit," of which the final consummation is found in Christ. Robertson again states, "Finally, the theme, 'I shall be your God and you shall be my people," reaches its climax through its embodiment in a single person. [28] Not in the tabernacle, but in Christ the covenant theme finds consummate fulfillment."[29] This fulfillment is found in His role as the High Priest over His people. Again Robertson states, "As kingly covenant-mediator, he does not administer the laws of the kingdom. It is **Himself** that he administers to His people. In the person of Jesus Christ, the covenants of God achieve incarnational unity."[30] The fact that the covenant mediator, which is Jesus, culminates in that Jesus Himself administers His life to His people so that He can incarnate Himself into them.[31] *"Such is the dramatic message of the uniqueness of the new covenant. An actual oneness with God himself is achieved through Jesus Christ the Son of God, as High Priest. He realizes the essential oneness between God and his people throughout history has been the ultimate goal of the covenant."*[32]

The main point of the fruit and culmination of the covenant is that God would establish a mutual oneness with His people. The sanctuary further points this out in the sacrificial offerings. As the sin offering represented Christ the offeror acknowledged to the offering that sin separated the two. And that by cutting the throat of the lamb (offering) it designated that the offeror had placed a substitute (i.e. the lamb) until the future culmination is met in antitype (i.e. Christ), of which represented the guilty heart of the offeror to strike or smite the lamb would bring about a sorry for sin and/or repentance of sin, even though it is not possible that the blood of bulls and of goats should take away sins.[33] This act, when offered with true heartfelt contrition, bonded the heart of man to Christ through the sacrifice. Further,

---

28. John 1:14; O. Palmer Robertson, *The Christ of the Covenants* (Phillipsburg, NJ: Presbyterian and Reformed Publishing, 1980), 50; see also Ephesians 2:21.
29. Ibid p.51.
30. Ibid p.52.
31. John 17:22, 23.
32. O. Palmer Robertson, *The Christ of the Covenants* (Phillipsburg, NJ: Presbyterian and Reformed Publishing, 1980), 296.
33. Hebrews 10:3.

still, the burnt offering sealed this conviction. As Gifford says, *"Many commentators believe that the chief function of the burnt offering was to atone for sin, but perhaps there was a different explanation. The sin offering dealt with sinfulness, so for the burnt offering to do the same would seem redundant. A second opinion is that the burnt offering was for a total surrender to God, or at least a willingness to do so, of the person making the sacrifice."*[34] H. Clay Trumbull describes the burnt offering as symbolizing *"the entire surrender to God, of the individual or of the congregation, in covenant faithfulness; the giving of one's self in unreserved trust to him with whom the offeror desired to be in loving oneness. It was an indication of a readiness to enter fully into that inter-union which the blood covenant had brought about between two who had been separated, but who were henceforth to be as one."* [35]

This sanctuary concept realizes the union of God with mankind through the sin and burnt offerings. First, the sin offering recognized the fact that the offeror needed atonement for sin and desired to become one with the sacrificial lamb. Second, the offeror realizes, through the burnt offering, his desire to become a "living sacrifice," as Paul said in Romans 12:1, desiring for His mutual inter-union, which is exactly what Jesus desired for mankind and which constituted much of His prayer in John 17.

The everlasting covenant, through love, was one that was based upon a mutual union between God and His people, both individually as the temple[36] and collectively as the body.[37] Sin is a breaking of this love-based covenant, a breaking of relationship. In a practical application, the Holy Spirit desires our union with Christ to be a moment-by-moment experience. We can now, by faith, participate in this union.[38] The fact that Jesus died and rose again so that we can die to self with Him and rise with Him in newness of life[39] is a daily experience, a moment-by-moment one that allows this mutual indwelling of each other[40] to take place. God even gives us the desire for this experience as Christ's purposes are carried out through us. Our encounters throughout each day will be Christ's divine appointments with others for redemptive purposes.

We just saw what God desires for His people, that they may be mutually

---

34. James D. Gifford, *Perichoretic Salvation* (Eugene, OR: WIPF Stock Press, 2011), 132-135.
35. H. Clay Trumbull, Blood Covenant, p. 249 as quoted in James D. Gifford Jr., Perichoretic Salvation, p. 134. Alfred Edersheim also agrees with this viewpoint in his book, The Temple, p. 93.
36. See 1 Corinthians 6:19.
37. See 1 Corinthians 12.
38. Ephesians 2:6 brings this out in the fact that we are now "sitting with Christ in heavenly places."
39. 2 Corinthians 5:21; John 5:24; Romans 5:9, 10, Romans 6:4,5,11.
40. John 17:22, 23.

> *An appreciation of God's character begets love, which begets true obedience.*

joined with Him, become healed and restored, and lead others to be healed and restored. As a matter of fact, God has already made the provision for this to happen on so many levels and He yearns to display His loving character to a dying world. An appreciation of God's character begets love, which begets true obedience. Ellen White expressed this sentiment: *"God deserves from all his creatures the service of love – service that springs from the appreciation of His character."*[41] It truly amazes me how easily the human heart can rationalize God's love away. If it weren't for God's Holy Spirit continually knocking upon our hearts and minds, how else could we stem the tide of complacency, rationalization, self-justification, mediocrity, lethargy, apathy, judgmentalism, and hedonism within our families, culture, and society as a whole?

God's motive has always been to mutually indwell Himself within us. When God's people abide in God and God in them, then what happens in heaven will happen on earth; thus does the kingdom come.[42] As we continue exploring, the next chapter deals with the fact that God has adopted us and that His desire for us is to be His free children and not enslaved servants of sin. We will see how He has brought about this process and that, through adoption, we can live under the dome where He is King. We then become intrinsically linked to a higher motive and purpose, which is to glorify God.

Thought Questions on the Kingdom's Love Covenant Gospel

1) What does the word "Christ" mean?

2) How does a denial of Christ's good news affect me?

3) What word is used for a person who denies Christ and his purpose and what does it mean?

4) In 1 John 2:20 what have believers been anointed to do?

5) Why is God's covenant based on love?

6) How is the gospel connected to God's love covenant?

---

41. Ellen White, *Patriarchs and Prophets* (Washington DC: Review and Herald Publishing Association, 1890), 34.
42. Matthew 6:10.

Kingdom of Adoption

**The human race already has been adopted in Christ,
please respond to your adoption!**

The mutual concept of Christ in His bride and the bride in Christ is foundational. This concept is God's revealed will for us, as Paul said in Colossians 1:27. Now we will look at how God has adopted us into this "oneness" with Himself.

The Greek word, even though it is not found in scripture, *perechoresis*, which means "mutual indwelling," is used to describe the relationship of the Trinity (Godhead). This concept, in which God has also allowed us to participate, is revealed throughout the New Testament. The key words in John 17:21, *"that they may be in us,"* are the most revealing, unbelievable, and powerful. Think of it—the God of the universe invites us into this *perechoretic* or mutually indwelling relationship with Himself! Now with this as the foundation, we will primarily focus on the idea of the adoption as sons and daughters into Christ.

When we become adopted into the kingdom through the Spirit, our purposes, goals, and desires become one with the Father, Son, and Holy Spirit.[43] We each still keep our individual identity, but have now been adopted with a specific purpose—glorifying God. Paul stated this clearly: *"For as many as are led by the Spirit of God, they are the sons of God. For ye have not received the spirit of bondage again to fear; but ye have received the Spirit of adoption, whereby we cry, Abba, Father. The Spirit itself beareth*

---

43. Ephesians 1:5; Romans 8:15-17.

witness with our spirit, that we are the children of God: And if children, then heirs; heirs of God, and joint-heirs with Christ; if so be that we suffer with him, that we may be also glorified together."[44] Paul is telling us that based upon our leading by the Spirit, our position and status have changed with God. Paul links it to the concept of redemption found in Galatians 4:4, 5. He states that Christ came to redeem us from being *under* the law. Now, I'm not saying that the law has been done away with; Paul clearly says that the law is established by faith and "God forbid" that we void the law.[45] However, God freed us from the bondage of sin so that *"we might receive the freedom of adoption of sons."* Paul reiterates that it was for this reason that we were given freedom: *"It was for freedom that Christ set us free."*[46] Therefore, through the Spirit, we are in Christ and Christ in us and have a true, experiential freedom by living in Christ, and this is what Paul defines as *'freedom'* and becoming a *'son of God.'* Becoming adopted into the kingdom is entering Christ by faith. However, what is even more marvelous is that Christ was slain from the foundation of the world, releasing all humanity from immediate condemnation. With that said, most don't realize that God has reconciled them and wasn't *"counting their sins against them."*[47] When we enter faith in Christ, the Spirit bears witness with us. John Stott says that the *"holy spirit testifies with our spirit that we are the sons of God – a witness he bears when, as we pray he enables us to cry, 'Abba Father', because we then know ourselves to be God's justified, reconciled, redeemed, and beloved children."*[48]

God broke down the barrier of sin (broken relationship), which He promised He would do from the beginning,[49] and through this reconciliation, we became grafted into the family as adopted heirs of Christ. Entering adoption, we have become reconciled[50] and live under the dome or domain of the King. God sets forth His life and imparts to us His sanctifying power, setting us free so that we may glorify Him. J. Billings brings this out: *"God's legal act of adopting into the family of God results in a new identity.... Thus when we are given an identity in Christ, we are called to live into it. The adopted identity in Christ, sealed by the Spirit, leads to living "for*

---

44. Romans 8:14-17.
45. Romans 3:31.
46. Galatians 5:1, NET.
47. 2 Corinthians 5:19, ISV.
48. John W. Stott, *The Cross of Christ* (Downers Grove, IL: Intervarsity Press, 1986), 213.
49. Genesis 3:15; Ephesians 2:14.
50. Ephesians 2:13-16.

the praise of His glory."[51] Therefore, our ultimate identity and purpose for our adoption into Christ is to live for the praise of His glory and character.

Furthermore, when we become children (sons and daughters) of God, then the spirit of fear vanishes. *"For you did not receive the spirit of slavery leading again to fear, but received the Spirit of adoption, by whom we cry, 'Abba Father'."*[52] If fear is gone, then we can know that perfect love has done the work of removing fear. We can say that the one who fears is in bondage and not truly free.

> **If fear is gone, then we can know that perfect love has done the work of removing fear.**

I have no intention of ever going bungee-jumping. I think that people who do it want to see how it feels to cheat death. Of course, death is only cheated if the bungee cord holds firm. I'm sure that some jump off feeling perfectly confident that the cord will hold while others jump fearing that the cord may not hold. Are there fears in life? You know that there are, and the fears are too numerous to count.

Some fears are healthy, such as the fear that might lead you to reject bungee-jumping, but when we are in Christ, we have the privilege of overcoming all unhealthy fears. When we enter into Christ, we become adopted into the Godhead. Paul says that when this happens we, as little children, can cry, "Abba Father." This idea comes from Greek and Roman cultures. When a family wanted to adopt a slave as a son, the adopted son took the father's name and was regarded as the true son and heir of the father. He now had the right to call his former master his father, whereas previously he had no right to do so. Romans 8:17 says that we become *'joint heirs with Christ.'*[53] Adopted Roman children, under the law, had the same inheritance rights as birth children. When a biological or adopted child cries "Abba Father," the idea is that the parent will always protect and do what is best for that child. By faith, we may experience this privilege of calling God our Father because He has claimed us as His own.

Giving Christ the permission to enter us is a daily privilege, and the experience begins with our first conscious breath in the morning and continues as a moment-by-moment experience throughout the day. Paul mentions this as a continuum throughout our day by praying without ceasing,

---

51. J. Todd Billings, *Union with Christ* (Grand Rapids, MI: Baker Books, 2011), 19, 20; see also Ephesians 1:11, 12.
52. Romans 8:15, NET.
53. See also John 15:15; Galatians 4:7.

walking in the spirit, dying daily, etc.[54] As Christians and children of the King, we need to wake up and realize that every moment of our lives is a surrendered moment. Through God's love, all of us are asked to choose this high calling.

Let me repeat this point: being in a love-covenant relationship with God as our Father is a continual surrendering of our lives to Christ. This surrender is not a one-time thought or act. It's a moment-by-moment, lifetime surrender.

The only life that we have to live is composed of the present. Jesus said in John 8:31 to continue in His word. "Dwell," "remain," "abide," "continue," and "occupy" are just a few of the words that describe the abiding presence of Christ in us. The degree to which we allow Christ in us is the degree to which the Spirit of God bears fruit in us, and it only happens when we consciously, on a moment-by-moment basis, yield to Him. To the extent that we do this is the extent to which we become the body of Christ, bearing much fruit. This moment-by-moment experience allows us to continually dwell in Christ. Therefore, to the extent that I'm awake to the Spirit I will be dead to self.

Isaiah describes how God consistently holds onto us: *"Fear thou not; for I am with thee: be not dismayed; for I am thy God: I will strengthen thee; yea, I will help thee; yea, I will uphold thee with the right hand of my righteousness."*[55] This verse tells us that God takes the initiative to take care of us, and Paul says that we can be *"confident of this very thing, that He that began a good work in you will perform it until the day of Jesus Christ."*[56] We need to have faith that He is working in us. Faith is not based upon how I feel, what I see, what I hear, or my circumstances and situations, because those can change. Rather, faith is based on a principle of what we know is true about God throughout His word. There are several examples in Scripture, but let us look closely at the text in Isaiah. In Isaiah, God is holding my hand. I'm not holding His hand. If I were holding His hand, I would let it go, or my hand would slip.[57] If I walk away from God, He, through the Spirit, nudges me to convict me that I will only be causing myself and Him pain. It doesn't mean I can't leave, but rather He draws me back to Him. Also, circumstances in our lives could cause us to let go of God's hand, but as we walk in Him, He confirms that there is no need

---

54. 1 Thessalonians 5:17; Galatians 5:16; 2:20.
55. Isaiah 41:10.
56. Philippians 1:6, AKJV.
57. Isaiah 41:10, 13.

to fear. Our response to realizing that He holds us is to have faith in what He says without doubting.

James says that when people doubt what God says, it's like they are a wave that is tossed about to and fro, not knowing where they are going.[58] The waves guide the direction in which we move. Therefore, when people ride a wave, they are helpless to the extent that they are moved in the direction of the wave and are powerless to govern the direction of their lives. However, based upon God's Word, we should have no doubt, and it is through entering by faith into the kingdom that our lives are directed through faith in His Word. Let's look at another verse regarding faith: "Likewise reckon ye also yourselves to be dead indeed unto sin, but alive unto God through Jesus Christ our Lord."[59] The King James Version uses "reckon"; some versions say *"consider."* Both words are faith words. In other words, some days in my life I might not feel "dead to myself and alive to God," but again we don't base our relationship with God on how we feel. Rather, I consider that I am dead, despite how I feel. If our feelings battle us, we should pray to God and ask Him for His faith.

Paul even equates fear with timidity. Paul says to Timothy: *"For God hath not given us the spirit of fear; but of power, and of love, and of a sound mind."*[60] Paul admonishes Timothy that God has given him power, love, and self-control (sound mind). These are the opposite of fear. The Greek word that is usually used for fear is *phobias*. However, Paul doesn't use that word here; he uses the word *deilia,* meaning "timid and cowardly." Even Revelation lists *"cowards"* as not receiving the kingdom. Living under the dome in which God reigns means that there is no room for being timid or cowardly.[61] If Galatians 5:6 says that *'faith is worketh by love,'* the Greek word for "worketh" in the KJV is actually *energeo,* which would mean that faith is energized or motivated by love, and if perfect love casts out fear, whether it be *phobias* or *deilia,* then to the degree that we live under God's dome, there will be the absence of fear and timidity. As darkness is the absence of light, so fear is the absence of love. Because we have entered Christ, we have entered His life, and there was no fear in Christ's life.

As sons and daughters of God, being adopted into the life of Christ, we can realize the impact that the life of Christ plays within our lives and roles as Christians. If the world sees the life of Christ in His body[62]

---

58. James 1:6.
59. Romans 6:11.
60. 2 Timothy 1:7.
61. Revelation 21:8 lists 'cowards' as those who do not enter into the kingdom.
62. 1 Corinthians 12:14.

collectively as the church, then we individually experience Christ as the temple. The continual, mutual indwelling (*perecherosis*) that God desires for His bride needs to be and will be, the desire of all who follow Him to be like Him. The beautiful thing is that when God writes His law (character) upon our hearts,[63] He is doing it within us and through us. To the extent that this happens is the extent to which we get out of the way and allow Christ to have His way in us.

Just as beautiful as that is, God never leaves us during the process, though we may fall. Hebrews 10:14 states that "by one offering he has perfected (made complete) forever those who are being sanctified." As we live the Christian life, God sees us in the process of being set apart, made holy, and sanctified in and for Him. Hebrews 2:11 echoes this concept as well: "For both he that sanctifies and they who are (being) sanctified are all of one: for which cause he is not ashamed to call them brethren". The Greek brings out the fact that this process of sanctification is an ongoing one, which Christ realizes and understands. The good news is that when He is being reproduced in our hearts, He doesn't forsake us, but rather calls us His brothers and sisters as we grow. In other words, it does not bring Him shame when we may struggle at times to live in this life by faith. Therefore, don't become discouraged if you go three steps forward and two steps back. Remember that the next time you struggle with life, He holds your hand, as we saw earlier, and helps you. He understands the process and knows the human heart; that is why Paul can say, "For since he himself has suffered when he was tempted he is able to give help (succor) to those who are tempted."[64] He has dived into humanity, experiencing all the comparable problems that we experience. He is the God that is on the inside of the problems of our lives, not the outside.

God can provide help in time of need. *"Let us therefore come boldly unto the throne of grace, that we may obtain mercy, and find grace to help in time of need."*[65] God gives us grace in time of need through Christ. The hard part is to allow God to determine or define when that "time of need" is. The danger is when we assume when that "time of need" is and God doesn't come through for us per our assumption. When this happens, a strain is put on the relationship, and we may begin to redefine who God is based on this experience. Unfortunately, this happens with so many people. However, patience is needed for God to reveal when that time is. Job

---

63. Hebrews 8:10; Jeremiah 31:33.
64. Hebrews 2:18, NET.
65. Hebrews 4:16.

was starting to go in that direction, without patience, until God revealed to Job the spiritual warfare that He was dealing with in this world. We can expect that God answers all prayers, but let's not evaluate how or when God does it. Job nearly gave in to this concept when God came to him and revealed that he was *"darkening God's counsel with words without wisdom."* Job took the advice and became speechless by putting his hand over his mouth.[66] This example teaches me that I must stop trying to redefine who I think God truly is.

Several years ago, my wife and I adopted a little girl from China. She was sixteen months old when we went to China to get her. On the day of her adoption, she had a difficult time letting go of her caretakers and accepting us as her adopted parents. For the first week or so she was reluctant to let us into her world. She appeared confused and mad at times. I can only guess what her little mind was thinking, *who are these people and what is going to happen to me.* Due to the language barrier of her knowing only Mandarin and us knowing only English, we had to prove to her, through our actions, that we were going to love her and take care of her. As she experienced our caregiving, she realized that we were not going to hurt her and that our character towards her matched the fact that our love and concern was for her. Not only did she begin to smile and laugh, but about six weeks after her adoption, she began to love and show affection toward us. When she was about four years old she said, "you were flying around and around the world and you found me; I am glad to be in this family." She is still aware and appreciative of us adopting her. I cannot help but think how other children in the world just like her need that same adoption experience. In my eyes, orphanages should be empty today based upon our Christian ideology. *"Pure religion and undefiled before God and the Father is this, to visit the fatherless and widows in their affliction, and to keep himself unspotted from the world."*[67] The word "visit" in this passage is not how we would interpret it. The Greek brings out the fact that there is action behind the word. In other words, it denotes tending to their needs or taking care of them, since most all widows and orphans are afflicted. The major point that James conveys is that widows have no husband and orphans have no father. The existence of these social outcasts provides the character of the Father and Husband in the absence of the father and husband in their lives thus revealing the character of God to them.

In first-century Roman culture, social issues were distorted. Most

---
66. Job 40:4.
67. James 1:27.

women were at significant disadvantages, but being a widow or an orphan compounded the problem. If a widow owed money to the Roman government and she could not pay it back, then her land was confiscated, or she was forced to become a prostitute or a slave. Unless someone else would take her in, there weren't many options for her. If a family owed money and there was no way to pay it back, the Romans would take a child from the family for slave labor. Orphans often became slaves in Roman society. If there were no natural descendants to the family line, then adults could be adopted in order to keep the family name or ancestry line going.[68] James saw these needs in the first century church and in Roman society and that is why he was concerned with the *"pure religion"* of Christianity.

As we relate to being adopted into God's family, which is another way that God has ascribed worth to the human race, we must recognize the fact that our job toward others is giving them the worth that God ascribes to them. To the extent that we become involved in recognizing the issue of displaying God to widows, orphans, and others that are afflicted, we fulfill an aspect of the commission of the three angels' messages. In relationship to the marginalized of society in the poor and suffering Ellen White states, "Christ on the mount of Olives pictured to His disciples the scene of the great judgement day. And He represented its decision as turning upon one point, when the nations are gathered before Him, there will be but two classes, and their eternal destiny will be determined by what they have done or have neglected to do for Him in the person of the poor and the suffering.[69] If we were honest with the text of the first angel's message in Revelation 14:6, 7, we can see that the everlasting gospel ascribes glory to God, who is the Creator of all. In other words, the everlasting gospel shows forth or puts on display the character of God, especially when we act toward others as God acts towards us. God the Creator is revealed in His glory or character. In a similar manner, "…another angel come down from heaven, having great power; and the earth was lightened with his glory."[70] This angel comes to earth, and the earth was *lighted* (*photoizo*—from where we get the word "photograph") or made to see his glory or character. Therefore, to the extent the gospel is lived out is to the extent the world will see the character of God put on display through His people, His body.

God had already set in motion the adoption papers in foreshadowing

---

68. J.A. Cook, *Law and Life of Rome 90 B.C.-212 A.D.* (Ithica, NY: Cornell University, 1984), 112.
69. Ellen G. White, The Desire of Ages (Mountain View, CA: Pacific Press Publishing Association, 1911), 637.
70. Revelation 18:1.

His death from the foundations of the earth.[71] When we, by faith, recognize our adoption, our daily battle against unbelief intensifies and never ends, resulting in spiritual warfare. However, when we become more settled into the truth a sealing process occurs. Within this spiritual warfare, our duty is to die daily so that we don't judge others. If self doesn't die, it projects judgment on others. Social evaluation escalates within the unregenerate heart. Not judging others, even though others may judge us, is living God's love. Francis Schaeffer said, "the world has a right to look upon us and make a judgment. Jesus tells us that as we love one another, the world will judge, not only whether we are his disciples, but whether the Father sent the Son. The final apologetic, along with the rational, logical defense and presentation, is what the world sees in the individual Christian and in our corporate relationships together."[72] Dietrich Bonhoeffer said, "By judging others we blind ourselves to our own evil and to the grace which others are just as entitled to as we are."[73] We should ask ourselves these questions: Does Christ shine through me? Is the world seeing God in me? Do I put Christ on every day for Him to shine through? To the extent that I do this is the extent to which I live under His dome. The cosmic conflict runs deep, and the comparison is between the highest good of character and the lowest evil of character. Tonstad states, "God's method is crucial in the drama. Since the issue in the conflict revolves around the kind of person God is, the winner of the battle is not determined simply on the basis of power and might. ...the antagonist in the conflict cannot be brought to heel by force. The deceiver must be unmasked, and the task of doing that has in Revelation been accomplished by Jesus in the form of a Lamb that looks 'as if it had been slaughtered' (5:6). This lamb is the definitive manifestation of God's character in history. ...the twofold mission of unmasking the deceiver on his own terms and of unveiling what God is like in a way that wins the confidence and admiration of the entire universe. Evil must be magnified to its fullest before being destroyed forever."[74]

The universe will see two opposite polarizations of character—supreme evil in comparison to the greatest love of God displayed in an adopted, reconciled, redeemed, people who choose to live moment-by-moment under the dome in which God reigns. In the end, the universe will forever see that God is love. This is the defining point of God's character

---

71. Revelation 13:8.
72. Francis A. Schaeffer, *The God Who is There* (Downers Grove, IL.: Intervarsity Press, 1968), 152.
73. Dietrich Bonhoeffer, *The Cost of Discipleship* (New York: Simon and Schuster Publishing, 1995), 185.
74. Sigve K. Tonstad, *Savings God's Reputation* (New York: T&T Clark, 2006) 346.

and our adoption. Ellen White put it this way: *"The great controversy is ended. Sin and sinners are no more. The entire universe is clean. One pulse of harmony and gladness beats through the vast creation. From Him who created all, flow life and light and gladness, throughout the realms of illimitable space. From the minutest atom to the greatest world, all things, animate and inanimate, in their unshadowed beauty and perfect joy, declare that God is love."* [75]

Thought Questions on the Kingdom of Adoption

1) How has Christ adopted us?

2) When did we become adopted?

3) What does God continually do, through Christ, for us as adopted children?

4) When Christ dwells within us, what privileges do we have as his adopted children?

5) As adopted children, what is our inheritance?

6) How does Christ release us from fear?

7) How does my adoption produce all of the qualities of Christ in me?

---

75. Ellen G. White, *The Great Controversy* (Mountain View, CA: Pacific Press Publishing Association, 1911), 678.

Kingdom of Holiness

The Lord's Prayer states that God's name is holy. The Greek word for "holy" is *Hagidzo*, meaning "sanctified, or separated." This means that God's name is to be separated and consecrated for a special purpose and recognition. In other words, God is the opposite of common. Worldly things are "common." John 1:10 states that the "world did not know Him" and that's because He was separate from the world, consecrated from the world. He wasn't recognizable by the world, because when people are conditioned to darkness, thinking it's light, then when light comes, it's labeled as darkness.[76] Because He taught His disciples how to differentiate between these two opposites, God's kingdom took on a different perspective.

The beautiful thing is that because God is *holy* and not *common*, the promise is that we can be as well—*"as he was in the world so are we."*[77] God designs that His people become separate for a higher calling in this life. Be the light in the world. We don't need to live for this worldly kingdom: rather, we can be fully awake and aware of separating ourselves from the world for His holy purpose. Anything less is to desecrate Him. We desecrate something when we take something holy and make it common or worldly. Usually, our human nature feels less guilty and more comfortable when we bring holy things down to our level. Our nature desires to bring

---

76. John 3:17-21.
77. 1 John 4:17, WEB; 1 Peter 1:16.

holy things down to a human level, because it makes people feel less guilty and God more *common*. When this happens, God's beauty diminishes in His people, and it becomes hard to distinguish between God's people and the world. However, God came down to our level to lift us up to Him and incorporate us into His life as representatives of the church, the living body.

Romans 6 teaches us to die to self in order to receive His new life. Also, Peter says, *"Be holy in every aspect of your lives, just as the one who called you is holy because it is written you are to be holy for I am holy."*[78] Peter is saying, in essence, that we are to reflect God's holiness and uniqueness in our lifestyles and characters.

As we are mutually dwelling in Him, we become separate from the world. However, as we become more distinct from the world, it doesn't make us haughtier; rather, we become holy in Christ and become ministers of reconciliation, reconciling people while beside them, not *over* them. As humility is a fruit of agape love, we become consecrated to a different Master. Peter further says that we are "a spiritual house built with living stones to be a holy priesthood and to offer spiritual sacrifices that are acceptable to God."[79] Because of Christ's death, through the Spirit we align ourselves with God, and when we do, we become a royal priesthood, just as the Levitical priesthood was set apart for spiritual services to God, offering spiritual sacrifices.

The Levitical priesthood had a consecrated and separate calling, making them unique and special. As much as they had a special calling on their lives, so do we, insofar as we are called to become a consecrated, called out, dedicated, and separate people that God uses in a distinct way. As compared to the daily priestly offering, we make spiritual sacrifices and also our sacrificial offerings are as living praise offerings. Paul states, "offering the sacrifice of praise to God continually giving... thanks to His name."[80] Therefore, as much as we are called to pray without ceasing, walk in the Spirit, and receive the mind of Christ on a continual basis, we are to give God the glory and thank Him for what He has done. The way that we live sacrificially with our time, talents, and physical resources for our friends and enemies sets us apart from the world of self-serving. It sets us apart for a high and holy calling. We become a distinct people called to a different purpose of life. Peter says, "you are a chosen race."[81] We became a chosen, new, human race that God has given as a priesthood to exemplify His character to the world.

---

78. 1 Peter 1:15, 16, ISV.
79. 1 Peter 2:5, NET.
80. Hebrews 13:15, WEB.
81. 1 Peter 2:9, WEB.

He tore down that wall that separated us, as Ephesians 2 states, and created a new human race through the cross. As kingdom people, we are a unique, called out, holy race, glorifying God through the character of Christ in our lives. We've been set apart for a singular purpose, living and talking in such a way that God's mighty acts are lived out. The law of love is displayed in God's people. When this happens in us, it exemplifies the truth in Christ, thereby making it attractive to people; or it can repel people. To the extent that Christ came down to reach us is the same extent to which we reach out to others.[82]

As Jesus is in us, we become more patient, have more peace, relate to others as Jesus did, ascribe value to all humans, withhold judgment of others, and love those who hate and use us. It becomes our one distinct calling—that the fullness of Christ is displayed before a dying world. In Revelation 18:1 an angel brings a message so that the whole world is enlightened or "made to see" (*photizo*). God's glory reflects in the lives of His followers through the power of the message that the angels brought down. Is it any wonder then that God waits for His people to accept this high calling? Joel 2 speaks of a risen people as a powerful army. Peter also says, *"once you were not a people, but now you are God's people... but now have obtained mercy."*[83] It was God's mercy that empowered a people who were willing to become changed. Our identity is given to us by God because we recognize that He owns us, and when that rings true, we will see ourselves as aliens and act as exiles in the world. Why? Because the world is opposite of our true identity. It's not an overnight experience, and many times our human nature gets in the way of the process of what God desires. However, if God receives the praise, despite how we feel, we can then rejoice for what He desires, because it's not about us or what we do, but rather what God has done and given to us for the privilege of being involved in His ministry.

True kingdom people are not linked to any other kingdom, nation, or political identity on this earth. Our identity is so linked to heaven because of the living Christ in us that we become foreigners, exiles, and strangers in the world. We wage war only against our flesh. Paul says, *"You therefore must endure hardness, as a good soldier of Jesus Christ. No soldier on duty entangles himself in the affairs of life, that he may please him who enrolled him as a soldier."*[84] He reminds us that we are soldiers and that the flesh is the false way of living. The flesh way of living is living out of our self-interests and

---

82. Philippians 2:5-8.
83. 1 Peter 2:10, NHEB.
84. 2 Timothy 2:3,4 WEB.

desires. It's rooted in thought patterns such as *What's in it for me, my nation, my worldview and my political ideology?* Our new identity is always based on Christ displayed on the cross. We are called to resist the pull of the affairs of this life and the *common*, self-gratifying desires of this world.

Therefore, the shift is that our decisions should not then be based on our self-interests, but rather in the interests of the kingdom of God. I know what you're thinking—*easier said than done*—right? There's only one simple faith experience that God asks of us, and that is to die daily. Every day, every moment, and every second. Even when we don't *"feel"* like it. Tell God that you don't feel like it and ask Him to give you the desire to come to Him. That is where faith comes in. Faith is not based on feeling, but principle. Faith is based upon not what I did, but what God did in Christ Jesus. Romans 5:1 says that we are "justified by faith, therefore we have peace." Therefore, it doesn't matter how I feel. It is by faith, despite how I feel. I can have peace despite my circumstances or situations. If you need the desire or feeling to die to self, God will give you that as well.

Accessing God's peace is by faith. In many situations, Jesus felt that same pull toward anxiety and unrest in His life, as did Elijah and many others. God desires us to be honest and authentic with Him. Despite how we feel, God can surpass our feelings. Again, giving God the permission to come into our lives so that He can live His life through us is the key. To the degree we allow God to do this is the degree to which we are inviting His presence to come in, and we can participate in His peace, mercy, grace, and compassion. There is an old painting of Jesus knocking on the door, which is based on Revelation 3:20 and reflects His desire for the mutual indwelling of which He spoke in John 17:23. I remembered that there was no handle on the door. God desires to dwell within us, but He never uses coercion or force to make it happen. He even initiates the knocking! Paul realized the fact that when we die to self, God lives authentically in us.[85] To the degree we experience this, Paul says we imitate or mimic Christ,[86] all the while growing in His love. This is our high, holy, consecrated calling. With every heartbeat, thought, and action, we are to receive and manifest the kingdom of God, which is based on love. All of the attributes of the Spirit—love, joy, peace, longsuffering, compassion, patience, etc.—are based on God's love. Love is not only the verb that God does but the noun that He is. By receiving the action of love as it takes place in our lives,[87] we become a channel for God to

---

85. Galatians 2:20.
86. 1 Corinthians 4:16.
87. 1 John 4:8; Galatians 5:22, 23.

display Himself in and through us. Insomuch as we allow this, we submit ourselves to the King and manifest the kingdom of God. When people submit, it implies that they become submissive or humble. Only people who submit to another agree that they recognize and bring their allegiances to the other's authority. Therefore, by beholding Jesus, we become like Jesus. In receiving His life, we manifest that life toward others. Ellen White stated, *"It is a law both of the intellectual and the spiritual nature that by beholding we become changed. The mind gradually adapts itself to the subjects upon which it is allowed to dwell. It becomes assimilated to that which it is accustomed to love and reverence."*[88] As we become more consistent in that, we stand out in the world and become more separate and holy in comparison to those who live out their self-interests.

> *Love is not only the verb that God does but the noun that He is.*

Jesus's life proved that it's not a common thing to be separate, and when we live in God's best interests, we will stand out. As we manifest His life, it convicts and attracts those who are hungering and thirsting for the kingdom, and at the same time and at the same time it repels others. Like a mustard seed, the kingdom grows by a genuine and real love for others. As people see that it's real and genuine and not just superficial and pacifistic, God's love convicts them. God's kingdom is a selfless one, and it always looks like Jesus dying on the cross for his enemies.[89] By upholding this thought, we will never forget that the kingdom progresses in the opposite manner of our selfish natures.

So far as this is manifested, the kingdom is manifested and grows exponentially. The early church caught this vision, and they were willing to go to the coliseums and hippodromes in vast numbers for their faith. The Jews saw this and stated, *"these that have turned the world upside down…"*[90] True kingdom living in the eyes of the world not only doesn't make sense, but it appears crazy. Participating in Christ's kingdom is trusting God to meet our needs, turning the other cheek, praying for our enemies, and sacrificing for others. Stand out from what is common. Don't look to others for what the kingdom is supposed to look like; that only leads to judgment and self-righteousness. Instead, look to Christ and imitate Him because the kingdom always looks like Him.

---

88. Ellen White, *The Great Controversy* (Mountain View, CA: Pacific Press Publishing Association, 1911), 555.
89. Romans 5:8, 10.
90. Acts 17:6.

The Phillips version of Romans 12:2 says, *"don't let the world squeeze you into its mold."* So many times we get our worldview from the news on TV or social media, choose political slants for this reason or that, and formulate ethical issues based on the media. We respond with behaviors such as obtaining guns to protect ourselves or removing ourselves from people by living farther away or building bigger and better houses, slowly conforming to wanting bigger, better, more, and "needing" this or that. Many of these issues in our lives are usually based upon fear. Some of these are not necessarily bad, but we shouldn't expect fulfillment from them. And above all we should never allow the world to mold our picture of God.

Whatever political, national, or ethical system, no matter how good they appear, they don't look like Jesus. True Christianity can never be nationalized, politicized, or ethicized because all the kingdoms of this world are under the influence of Satan.[91] Everything is at stake in regards to preserving the holiness of God in His people. If not, then His name becomes desecrated, and His people lose their distinctive kingdom calling, inevitably forgetting that they are aliens and exiles in the world. Through a daily beholding of Christ, we prevent our lives from slipping into commonality and from rationalizing truth away. Commonality will still allow us to hold onto our profession of Christ. However, if we're not allowing a mutual indwelling with Him, then we will begin to walk down the road of self-deception.[92] When this happens, we have recreated God in our minds rather than Him recreating our minds in His image. It also mingles our self-interests with the interests of the kingdom of God. We fuse worldly causes with God's causes and lose our distinctiveness and ability to recognize the difference. There is a constant pull of the world against The Kingdom, which leads to being conformed to the world instead of being transformed by the renewing of our minds.[93] We need to be cognizant of this aspect of the spiritual war in which we are engaged.

When the devil offered Jesus all the kingdoms of this world in exchange for worship, Jesus could have given in and had them all. However, Jesus didn't dispute that Satan had all the kingdoms of this world.[94] If Jesus complied with Satan, Satan would have perhaps stepped back from the spiritual pull he had on mankind and Jesus' message of peace, righteousness, and holiness would have had a better opportunity to be received, and the promised healings

---

91. See Revelation 17:8; 18:3; 1 John 5:19; Ephesians 2:2.
92. James 1:6-8; 22 .
93. Romans 12:2.
94. 1 John 5:19, Revelation 17:8; 18:3.

would have poured forth through the messianic anointing spoken of in Isaiah 61:1-3. But then Satan is a liar and this would most likely never have happened. However, Jesus would not compromise the kingdom or His holiness for the false exchange—and again Satan is the Father of Lies. The promise of Isaiah 61 would still be fulfilled, but only by beholding a sacrificial love that held Jesus on the cross. He allowed the kingdom powers of this world to crucify Him. By coming under the world through love and not over it through a coercive conformity, He won the world unto Himself. That is the holiness of God's kingdom. God's love leads us under the dome in which Jesus is the King. Jesus conquered the world by saving it from the inside outward, rather than from the outside inward. He planted a different and distinct kingdom that doesn't look like any other kingdom of this world. True love never coerces to grow its kingdom. Jesus exchanged any short-term gain of temporary peace offered by Satan for the long-term plan of God's love, which in the end would rule throughout eternity. Unfortunately, the church has succumbed to the very temptation that Jesus resisted. Church history is proof that the kingdom-over method operated through force and violence, and even Jesus recognized that those leaders who desired their religious ways to be viewed as correct used force on the people.[95]

> ***True love never coerces to grow its kingdom.***

When God's kingdom is displayed through his church, His love is shown to the world. The radical idea of agape love is that it draws and compels through honoring people rather than coercing people. That is the holiness of God's kingdom. To the degree that this does not happen, God's people lose their distinctive character, default into a pluralistic culture, and blend into the world. Our holy authority is to provide service to others, and our job is not to police, judge, fix, or legislate the morality of the world. God's command is to love the world, wash their feet, feed them, and cloth them. These attributes of agape love give the unique message of a people who receive His righteousness by faith. The first angel's message, found in Revelation 14:6 and 7, displays this everlasting gospel. Our allegiance to Christ has to be incomparably greater than our allegiance to a nation, political party, or our opinions. We must always remember that we are exiles in the world. As we are exiles in the world, we are to be lights that shine in the world. Isaiah states, "Arise, shine; for thy light is come, and the glory (character) of the LORD is risen upon thee for, behold, the darkness shall cover the earth, and gross darkness the people: but the

---

95. See Matthew 11:12.

LORD shall arise upon thee, and his glory (character) shall be seen upon thee. And the Nations shall come to your light and kings to your bright light."[96] As exiles, the promise is sure that God is glorified. As Paul stated, "Now then we are ambassadors and representatives for Christ, …be ye reconciled to God."[97] When God reconciles people, Jesus is revealed.

As God's representatives, we are created in His image. As Jesus held up a coin in Luke 20:24 and 25, with the image of Caesar on it, He compared it with the image of man. Jesus said, *"Show me a penny. Whose image and superscription does it have? They answered and said, Caesar's. And he said unto them, then give therefore unto Caesar the things which are Caesar's, and unto God the things which be God's."* Even though on the surface Jesus is talking about financial responsibility and stewardship, however spiritually Jesus is contrasting images. Jesus was saying, give back the money to Caesar, and give back the image of God and put it back into man. Jesus is more interested in the formation of the correct image of God in man thereby reflecting a people group who are representatives of God on earth. Paul spoke of being conformed to the image of His Son.[98] That is why we become temples of God, as Corinthians states,[99] so that God can form a body of believers that look like Jesus in the world.[100]

Thought Questions on the Kingdom of Holiness

1) What does "holy" mean?

2) What do I need to do daily to receive God's holiness?

3) Why does God need a separated and holy people?

4) How does living under the dome of the King affect how I relate to others?

5) How can we become honest and authentic with God and others?

6) How can we align our minds more with God's purposes?

7) In what way does the world squeeze us into its mold?

---

96. Isaiah 60:1-3.
97. 2 Corinthians 5:20.
98. Romans 8:29.
99. 1 Corinthians 6:19.
100. 1 Corinthians 12:12-14.

A Kingdom of Priests

We touched upon the priesthood in the previous chapter and saw that it was always God's intention to develop a people that would impart the gifts of His righteousness in Christ upon all believers through a priesthood. God desires His people to be an extension of Himself in the body and anoint those who not only desire healing and restoration in their lives but to deliver the gospel message to others as well. We saw in the first chapter that God had anointed a people for a special purpose to show His character through the gospel of healing and restoration.[101] Therefore, to realize what the priesthood entails, we will look at several concepts. One is to define the priesthood and its formation, and what was meant for the priestly office in regards to its role and function. Another is to describe the duties of the priesthood and, finally, to delve into the spiritual application of the priesthood and how it affects our lives as Christians.

In linguistically examining "priest," the Hebrew word *kohen* (ko-hane') means "to mediate" and the Greek word *hiereus* (hee-er-yooce') means "sacred or holy." "The central concept of priesthood is mediation between the sphere of the divine and the ordinary world, or the holy and the common world. The priests represented God to the people in their clothing, their behavior, in oracles and instruction, while in sacrifice and intercession

---

101. 2 Corinthians 1:21; 1 John 2:20; Hebrews 1:9.

they represented the people to God."[102] The priesthood in the Old Testament is first mentioned as a compilation of people based upon the Levites being faithful to God. They were chosen based on what the Levite tribe did regarding their action against sin, in the camp of the Israelites, when Aaron constructed the golden calf.[103] The tribe of Levi came to God's aid as it related to cleansing the Israelite camp from this sin. This act led to the Levites becoming the tribe that would be used in an intermediary role for Israel. Therefore, a priesthood was born.[104]

Because the tribe responded to God's call for consecration, God chose them instead of the firstborn,[105] and they were to execute all services as it was related to the temple.[106] They were presented before the High Priest (Aaron being the first to fill this role).[107] The public consecration had deep spiritual applications. God commanded Moses to "sprinkle the water of cleansing on them and...wash their clothes and cleanse themselves."[108] Like baptism, the priesthood was to commit themselves to the Lord through this cleansing service. However, they were not to cleanse themselves. Moses, as a type of Christ, was appointed for that. Moses executed this role at the time even though Aaron became the first high priest. It was a symbolic act of regeneration. Paul echoed that duty of God for us.[109] This was not an ordinary, common bath, but a symbolic, spiritual cleansing. Only Moses, as a type of Christ, began the ministry of intercession and only God could clothe him with His righteousness.[110] As the priests were being consecrated with a sin and burnt offering,[111] they became the wave sheaf offering unto the Lord before the congregation of the people.[112] M.L. Andreason comments on this offering. "In this offering the Israelites said in effect, 'We have sinned and broken your covenant. We didn't repent and take our stand on your side when the call was made. We ask for your forgiveness and we acknowledge in choosing the tribe of Levites instead of our firstborn. We are not worthy to serve Thee God or to minister in Thy tabernacle. We present the Levites on our behalf. Accept

---

102. New International Dictionary of Old Testament Theology and Exegesis, Vol. 2, p. 600.
103. See Exodus 32:26-28.
104. See Exodus 38:21 and Numbers 1:50-53.
105. Numbers 3:7, 45.
106. Numbers 8:11, 3:7, 8.
107. Numbers 3:6, 9.
108. Numbers 8:6-9, NHEB.
109. Titus 3:5.
110. See Numbers 8:5-9, 11; Ps. 132:9.
111. Numbers 8:10-12, 20-22.
112. Numbers 18:11.

them, O Lord, as our offering.' God desired to make Israel a "nation of kingdom of priests, and a holy nation"[113] and their special prerogative as priests was that they may "draw near" to God."[114]

However, as previously mentioned, Israel, through their disobedience at Mt. Sinai, rejected God's offer to make them a kingdom of priests and broke God's covenant. "...instead of the whole nation's becoming a kingdom of priests, the tribe of Levi was chosen for that honor."[115] Even though only one tribe, the Levites, became the mediatorial tribe before God, God did not forsake His people or cancel out the nation of Israel as a people of the promise or the call that was made to Abraham.[116] God's call to Abraham was for Abraham to "walk before me and be thou perfect (complete)."[117] Therefore, as Israel accepted the Levites on "behalf of the people," Israel was accepted before God. "Israel might approach God through the ministration of those whom God appointed for the service."[118]

The anointing oil poured upon Aaron's head by Moses was an indication of the fullness of the Holy Spirit placed upon Aaron as he ministered before God.[119] Therefore, as Aaron was a high priest of the holy priesthood before God, so was Christ our forerunner as the High Priest before God.[120] The priesthood role and function was to intercede on behalf of the people as it was related to the transference of sin to the sanctuary. Therefore, to state it simply, the priesthood took the sin of an individual in the form of polluted blood through a sacrifice and presented it before God. Once a year the sanctuary was to be cleansed from the polluting sins and set right or justified once again. These transferences of sin were wiped clean by the true representation of Christ in the form of His sin offering. Therefore, the priestly function was to mediate and guide toward cleansing and restoring the individual to God. The fall feasts represented this—the Feast of Trumpets (*Rosh-sha-shanah*) warned the people to prepare for the cleansing of the sanctuary; then the Day of Atonement (*Yom Kippur*) arrived, upon which the cleansing happened, thereby setting right the sanctuary. Finally, the Feast of Tabernacles (*Sukkot*) represented the people in heavenly bliss.

---

113. Exodus 19:6.
114. M.L. Andreason, *The Sanctuary Service* (Hagerstown, MD: Review & Herald Publishing, 1947), 59.
115. Ibid. p. 60.
116. Genesis 12:1.
117. Genesis 17:1.
118. M.L. Andreason, *The Sanctuary Service* (Hagerstown, MD: Review & Herald Publishing, 1947), 60.
119. 1 Samuel 10:1; 6; 16:13; Isaiah 61:1; Luke 4:18; Acts 10:38.
120. Hebrews 2:17; 3:1; 4:14; 6:20.

Now as we consider the duties of the priest, we will do so from a pragmatic point of view. In other words, we won't go into detail about the development of the priesthood, but rather look at a list and brief description of each of its unique functional duties. They were direct functions of Christ, our High Priest, and representative of those gifts that were given to produce the fullness of Christ in His believers, as stated in Ephesians 3:19.

Here is the list, with corresponding verses.

1. **Priesthood and Firstborn**—Numbers 8:18 (Levites represent the firstborn)

    The Levites were representative of the priesthood because of their act against the golden calf in the wilderness and became the priesthood instead of the firstborn of Israel.

2. **Covenant of an Everlasting Priesthood**—Numbers 25:13

    God's covenant was based upon having an everlasting priesthood, one that symbolizes the spiritual metaphor of an unending people.

3. **Knowledge and Priesthood**—2 Chronicles 30:22

    The Levitical priesthood was to teach the "good knowledge of the Lord." In other words, the gospel would be spread through the priesthood, then the Israelites, and then the world.

4. **Purity of the priesthood**—Numbers 8:6, 15, 21

    The priests were to be representatives of God, pure and holy, which is the opposite of common and ordinary. This was accomplished through their cleansing and purifications, both inaugural and daily.

5. **Priests were rabbis (teachers)**—Deuteronomy 24:8

    The priests were to be teachers of righteousness, proclaiming the beauty of the sacrificial lamb to the people.

6. **Priests are the first fruits of Christ**—Nehemiah 10:37; Jeremiah 2:3

    The priesthood became God's first fruits of His increase because they became holy as He was. And through the priest Israel would become holy.

7. **Priests are anointed**—Exodus 28, 29, Leviticus 8, Exodus 29:7, 29

    The priesthood was anointed and given the unction of the Holy Spirit to function as God's representatives.

8. **Inaugurated into the sanctuary**—Leviticus 8

    The priesthood was inaugurated into the Sanctuary. In other words, they became a temple through which the Holy Spirit could work.[121]

9. **Priests receive new names**—Isaiah 62:2; Revelation 2:17; 3:12

    The priests received new names. God's holiness in them changed their characters. It was God's intention that new names represent new characters. Therefore, the new names were representative of their new roles and characters as God's priesthood and ambassadors.

10. **Imbued with the Holy Spirit**—Exodus 29:7, 29

    They were imbued with the Holy Spirit for making Israel holy thereby becoming ambassadors and a light to the surrounding nations.

11. **Priests teach**—2 Chronicles 3:22; 35:3; Nehemiah 8:9

    The priests were to be teachers and guides to Israel and the surrounding nations.

12. **Washing/baptism of priests**—Exodus 29:4; 30:20, 21; Exodus 40:31, 32; Leviticus 8:6; Eph. 5:26

    The priests were to daily wash each other with the word. Therefore it was both a physical and spiritual baptism.

13. **Wear white linen**—2 Chronicles 5:12; Zechariah 3:4; Revelation 19:8; Psalms 132:9.

    The priests wore white linen, which represented the purity and righteousness of Christ.

14. **Consecrated for 7 days**—Leviticus 8:33

    The high priest was consecrated for seven days, similar to Jewish

---

121. 1 Corinthians 6:19.

weddings where the groom and bride participated in the wedding feast that lasted seven days.

15. **Dedicated with blood**—Leviticus 8:24

    The high priest was dedicated with blood on the right ear, right hand, right thumb, and right foot and toe, all representative of a cleansing and sanctification process that is symbolic of the priest anointed in the sacrificial death of the lamb—to hear, do, and walk in the precepts of the Lamb.

16. **Have their hands "filled"**—Ezekiel 10:2

    The priest's hands are full of incense (prayer) and coals of fire (sacrificial offering). In other words, the priesthood should constantly be interceding on behalf of others and offering the sacrifice of praise in recognition of the death of Christ.[122]

17. **Holy Priesthood**—1 Peter 2:5; Numbers 3:3

    The priesthood is a holy priesthood, which implies that they are separated and sanctified from the world or common, ordinary things.

18. **They offer up themselves as a daily sacrifice**—Psalm 50:5; Psalm 51:17; 1 Peter 2:5

    The priesthood offers up sacrifices to God through humility with intercession, praise, consecration, solemnity, righteousness, and holiness. When Christ is in you, nothing is common or ordinary; rather, God's perfect love motivates you in bearing, believing, hoping, and enduring all things.[123]

19. **They are a spiritual temple**—1 Peter 2:5; 1 Corinthians 6: 19, 20; Eph. 2:19-22

    We as the priesthood become a temple wherein the Holy Spirit abides and dwells.

20. **They are living stones**—1 Peter 2:5

    The priesthood becomes living stones built upon the cornerstone.

---

122. Hebrews 13:15.
123. 1 Corinthians 5:14, 15; 1 Corinthians 13:7.

In other words, living stones are moving, breathing, rejoicing, praising, etc. The priesthood is made up of living stones because in Him *"we move live and have our being."*[124] It is a stone that is fully alive and yet fully reflective of Christ's indwelling. These living stones are transformed through His contact, receive His new life, and now become part of the edifice, a living body[125] that is built up into a living temple, declaring the deeds of God and His praises. However, they are solely dependent upon Christ to be made a living stone and continue to be part of the living temple. They have become a spiritual house and body a holy living priesthood, offering up spiritual sacrifices to God.

21. **Offering up spiritual sacrifices**—Psalm 51:17; 1 Peter 2:5

    The priesthood always offers up spiritual sacrifices because the sacrifice they offer is themselves as Romans 12:1 states that we become *"living sacrifices, holy, and acceptable to God, which is our reasonable spiritual service."* The priests were dedicated around the clock to the mediatorial service and edification of Israel. It was a full dedication that God desired of all His priesthood. David learned that our sacrifice to God is our broken spirit and a repentant heart.

22. **They are a holy nation**—Exodus 19:6; 1 Peter 2:9

    The priesthood becomes a holy nation that expands past the actual Levitical priesthood and anoints all the body of Israel. Even though that did not happen to national Israel, the promise that God will have a priesthood of all believers will come true.

23. **They are God's possession**—1 Peter 2:9; Ephesians 1:14

    God's priesthood is His possession. God never casts His people off and never forgets His inheritance as stated in Psalm 94:14.

24. **Royal priesthood**—1 Peter 2:9; Rev. 1:5,6

    God's righteous covenant, based on love, is renewed through a priesthood of all believers, through a description of the idea of becoming kings and a kingdom.

---

124. Acts 17:28.
125. 1 Corinthians 12.

25. **Offer intercessory prayers on behalf of others**—Ephesians 6:18; 2 Corinthians 1:11; Philippians 1:19; 1 Timothy 2:1

They offer intercessory prayers on behalf of others, as the daily priests did in the holy place before the altar of incense.

As 1 Peter 2:9 states, God has *"called out"* a chosen people. God has always waited for a priesthood that will reflect the goals, purposes, desires, and characteristics of their High Priest Jesus Christ. This could only happen as His priesthood is called out into His marvelous light.[126]

A major objective of the tabernacle in the wilderness was to set forth a pattern by which Christ has a living priesthood, in a living temple, offering up spiritual sacrifices. With the loss of the foresight of this, the system just became another ritual which would replace a deep experience on behalf of those who come to the temple. That's why Christ became the High Priest of the true tabernacle which the Lord pitched and not man. By accepting His death and receiving His life, believers become "living stones." The temple is a spiritual, living temple, built with "living stones" because God is spirit.[127] Its construction and cohesion are that of the sanctifying Spirit. Christ was "put to death according to the flesh, but made alive in the Spirit."[128] His glorified humanity gives to those who are united to Him the opportunity to be transformed by the Spirit in such a way that they become a temple of God and living stones built into the corporate spiritual sanctuary, a "spiritual house for a holy priesthood."[129] The idea of individuals built up as a priesthood into a body is the key to what Peter describes.[130] The idea is that as a corporate body, the priesthood seeks to glorify God. Peter describes the priestly character of the church in that it forms the temple of Christ. Therefore, we are individually a temple, but corporately the body of Christ.

The institution of the priesthood is a divine prerogative of Christ Himself. His sacrifice opened the door for the priestly service of all believers, even back in Exodus 19:6. It affirms a very close relationship between Christ and His priesthood. Christ *"has made priests"* and this affirms that Christ had the power to initiate this formation, which declares Him to be more than just a priest, because Christ as High Priest came from men.[131] Also, Christ has released mankind from their sins so that He may confer

---

126. Isaiah 60:1-3.
127. John 4:24.
128. 1 Peter 3:18, NHEB.
129. 1 Peter 2:9, NASB.
130. See also Ephesians 2:21, 22 and 1 Peter 2:3-5.
131. Hebrews 5:1.

priesthood upon them. Therefore, only Christ was able to allow fallen sinners to share in His relationship with the Father by bestowing upon them a priesthood which allows for an intimate relationship with the Father and Himself. The beautiful news is that as *'spiritual priests'* we have a *'mutual indwelling'* with Christ and the Father as is found in John 17:22, 23.

The institution of the priesthood is a divine prerogative of Christ Himself.

In Revelation 1:6 John reveals the divine promise fulfilled that began in Exodus 19:6. By means of His redemptive death, Christ has won for mankind a profound transformation from death to life, from sacrifice to priesthood. Now each Christian has become a living sacrifice through a meek and contrite spirit. This relationship, through Christ's redemptive death, has made them priests.

Those who enter by faith are Christian priests and have the privilege of entering the sanctuary and performing their priestly duties in relation to the last great conflict. The 144,000 have symbolically come from all twelve tribes and represent a royal priesthood.[132]

In Revelation 20:6 we can see that those who take part in the first resurrection have become priests unto God. Special attention is brought to view in that they are *"priests unto God and Christ."* Christ has bought these people *into* the priesthood and *unto* God. The new birth experience is attributed to what they have become—priests. This is a direct attribution to not only Christ, who has given them the new-birth life through His death and resurrection but also to the perpetuity of a living priesthood, which is in contrast to the priesthood where replacement is necessitated by ongoing death, as spoken of in Hebrews 7:23.

In Revelation 7:14, 15 we have a picture of a group of people who have come out of great tribulation, and they represent a very close connection between Christ and God. They are not only admitted into the sanctuary, which is a priestly prerogative, but they had the privilege of being before God day and night—a privilege not even afforded to the individual earthly priests. We notice two things about this group—1) in verse 14 they have robes made white because of Christ's life and 2) in verse 15 they minister before God day and night. The priestly robe is a holy one (Exodus 29:2) denoting a holy and set-apart priesthood. Christ has made them clean and fitted them for worship in His temple. They now have the privilege to *"minister"* to God day and night, just as the daily priests offered up

---

132. Revelation 7:4-8.

sacrifices, praise, and continual worship day and night.

What a compassionate, sharing God we have! He shares "power over the nations" as He "receive[s] it from the Father." He gives the "tree of life" for food.[133] He gives the "crown of life" to those who overcome as He did.[134] He gives the "hidden manna and the white stone" to those who overcome as He did. He will make those who overcome "pillars" in His temple, which refers to a priesthood. Ultimately He shares his throne with the overcomers.[135] Priests were the pillars that mediated between God and man in the Old Covenant tabernacle. Only to the priesthood are these privileges given and shared. Another aspect of the authority and duty of the priests, which is based on Deuteronomy 31:9-13, is that the divine law was given to the priests to make it known to all the people. The priesthood existed to serve and were to make the law a living and abiding presence of God's love. It is a gift of God which puts the priest at the service of his brethren. "For every high priest taken from among men is *ordained for men* in things pertaining to God, that he may offer both gifts and sacrifices for sins."[136]

The personal intimacy between the priests and their God is seen in Revelation 21:7, where God says, "I will be his God, and he shall be my son." The Sonship of Christ is so close that even God has adopted us as His sons and daughters. In Exodus 28:36, the high priest had written on his miter "holiness to the Lord." God's new priesthood also has that written, however, in their minds.[137] Their intimacy with God will surpass anything that an earthly priest or high priest had. As on the Day of Atonement, in which the high priest was in the presence of God one day a year, the new priesthood is before God, though in this case, day and night.[138]

VanHoye states, "As John had written that when Christians appeared as victims, criminals, and martyrs they, in reality, were both priests and kings. They had a privileged relationship with God that played a determining role in the history of the world! Their priestly royalty is presented as the culminating point in the redemptive work of Christ." [139] He further states, "Christ is the one who has brought about the complete union between mankind and God, for the benefit of all mankind. For this reason,

---

133. Revelation 2:7.
134. Revelation 2:10.
135. Revelation 3:21; 2:17; 10:1.
136. Hebrews 5:1, emphasis mine.
137. 1 Thessalonians 3:13.
138. Revelation 7:15.
139. A. VanHoye, *Old Testament Priests and the New Priest* (Petersham, MA: St. Bedes Publishing, 1980), 306.

the priesthood of Christ is fundamentally open to participation. Whoever is faithful to Christ is associated with the priesthood, for he finds in Christ an immediate relationship with God." [140] Christ's death and life brought about a new life and character that was infused into the priesthood.

There are two aspects to His offering. Christ put His whole existence at the disposal of God for the salvation of His brethren and the dissemination of His character. His offering is bringing about a perfect covenant between mankind and God, the redemption of humanity, a promotion to a priesthood, the vindication of God's character, and the solidification of His eternal Government. Therefore, by Him and His one offering, all can enter an intimate relationship with God.

The fact was that God's priests were to be a blessing to all. This is the main purpose around which Abraham's call was centered.[141] In fact, that blessing was to extend to Israel and all other nations.[142] Though this kingdom of priests, derived from Abraham, was to be a *'blessing'* to all nations around them, it failed.[143] Paul said that this gave the Christians the right to be both blessed and a blessing to everyone around them, thereby carrying on Abraham's call.[144] In other words, the people may have changed from national Israel to all who have individually received Christ, but the goal remains the same, and that is for Christians to bless others. The priesthood's focus is to be on others, not self.

When God allowed the Levites to become the priesthood, it was because they defended God's character and refused to become involved in the apostasy within the camp of the Israelites at the time. They were separating themselves for God, and that is what holiness and sanctification are all about. There was a juxtaposition of a separate and distinct people with a common, earthly people. They desired to be unique in God's character and 'set right' or 'justified' for God's eternal purposes. All of Israel were to be 'a kingdom of priests, a holy nation,' not just the Levites.[145] The fact that there remains a need for a priesthood to bless others, including their enemies, reinforces the fact that God's character is at issue in this cosmic conflict. God still seeks a people, a priesthood, that will bless others and ascribe, in a radical way, an unsurpassable worth toward others through which the Spirit transforms people from the inside out, making them a

---

140. Ibid., 313.
141. Genesis 12:2, 3.
142. Genesis 18:18.
143. Genesis 22:18.
144. Romans 4:9-25; 9:4-30; Galatians 3:6-29.
145. Exodus 19:6.

blessing toward others as well, thereby expanding His priesthood.

To sum up, the priesthood of the kingdom has its full realization in God's provision for all to enter through Christ into unity with His body of believers. When this happens, we become part of the spiritual priesthood that He ordained through His life, death, and resurrection. He has given unsurpassable worth to all humans and invites all to enter this marvelous, experiential sanctuary service. To the extent that this happens in an individual is the extent to which the priesthood becomes realized. The functions of the priesthood are selfless and fulfilling, ascribing unsurpassable worth to others, culminating in the revelation of God's true character to a fallen world. Only those who by faith have spiritually entered the holy place of the sanctuary would be a part of the ministry of priests and the priesthood of the sanctuary. Through the functions of the priest, they would then enter the most holy place. Each piece of furniture relates to a function in which each priest must participate. Each priest was to be of service to one another and all mankind. When this concept becomes true, then there will be a people united in God's covenant of love. What a beautiful and self-sacrificial picture of God! As we are under the domain of God, through knowing His love, we can have all the fullness of Christ to glorify Him.[146] Instead of giving us the judgment we deserve, God endlessly pours on us all blessings in Jesus Christ. Picture yourself as a rock below the Niagara Falls, and as it receives an endless overabundance of water on it, so God's love does the same for us. Paul says He lavishes on us all His riches.[147]

Thought Questions on the Kingdom of Priests

1) What is the Hebrew definition of the priesthood?

2) What are some of the functions of the priesthood?

3) How do we incorporate the duties of the priesthood into our work?

4) When and for what purpose did God call out His priesthood?

5) How can the priesthood better know the High Priest's purpose?

6) How do we ascribe unconditional worth to others?

7) In what ways can we, as God's priesthood, intercede for others?

---

146. Ephesians 3:19.
147. 1 Timothy 6:17.

Kingdom Awareness

We are created for the kingdom of God. The degree to which we behold the kingdom is the degree to that we are transformed by it. However, only knowing about the kingdom will not change us. There is a world of difference between knowing about something and knowing something, as much as there is between knowing a Bible verse about Jesus and living that Bible verse. To begin to understand the kingdom is to come to grips with the idea that you don't know the kingdom. The reason is that we as Christians have defined the kingdom under our terms rather than God's. In other words, social issues, social morals, and behavioral approaches to the kingdom that are presented from the pulpit have misaligned and thwarted the true faith that was once delivered unto the saints. Political and social issues were not uncommon in the first-century church with which Jesus dealt. However, He always brought people back to the true definition of the kingdom, especially as revealed in John 17.

If the kingdom looks like Jesus, then why do we see very little of Jesus in the church, let alone the world? If the problem can't be identified, then the solution to the problem will not be either. The problem will become ubiquitous or replaced with false solutions. Christians, for the most part, mirror the culture in which they live. Our society has an intangible yet profound component that makes us complacent and indolent. If we're not being transformed by the restoration and renewing of our minds, then by default we're conformed to the world around us. The 'renewing of the mind' through a 'transformation' of receiving Christ's mind allows us to be able to understand and know what is God's "good, acceptable and perfect will…" for our lives.[148] Therefore, the solution is to have a continually renewed mind in Christ. "Walking in the Spirit," as Paul says, is to be consciously aware of this fact all the time.

As we receive this new mind, a self-sacrificial love becomes the foundational mark of the kingdom. The myopic task for kingdom people is to replicate God's kingdom and love toward others while withholding all judgment and assessment of others. Above all our theology, ethics, cultural influences, and political standings, our continual thoughts are to be clothed with Jesus' self-sacrificing love. It is the greatest honor and highest thought to be likened to Jesus' love for enemies and identified with Him at this level. We must constantly battle our worldly, humanistic presuppositions of what the kingdom should look like. Paul says in 1 Corinthians 16:14 that everything we do should be done in love. The kingdom is pretty much opposite of every natural, human impulse that runs through our minds. Christ gives us the opportunity to live in opposition to what our natural tendencies are. To the degree we live this way, Christ is revealed, and to the degree we don't, we miss the mark, and worldly impulses take over. Paul said that the only thing that matters is faith that is established by love.[149] This Calvary love is what God uses to mold the church to look like Jesus, at every step defining who the church is. All the seminars, Bible studies, retreats, conferences, sermons, books read, and camp meetings attended have no value unless we live the kingdom and experience the value of allowing God's love to define us. God's love motivates so much that it bears, believes, hopes, and endures *all* things. However, as we unravel the love of God, it is only Christ in us that can love the unlovable, pray for our enemies, resist retaliation and judgment against others. This is the church's worst heresy—not allowing and developing the habit of putting Christ on every day, every minute, and every second. To the extent that the church does not do this, we can see both the church and the world quickly fulfilling 2 Timothy 3:1-5: "For men shall be lovers of their own selves, covetous, boasters, proud, blasphemers, disobedient to parents, unthankful, unholy, without natural affection, trucebreakers, false accusers, incontinent, fierce, despisers of those that are good, Traitors, heady, high-minded, lovers of pleasures more than lovers of God;

---

148. Romans 12:2.
149. Galatians 5:6.

Having a form of godliness, but denying the power thereof: from such turn away." Sounds pretty common in the church, doesn't it? It's the default mode when we don't allow Christ to dwell within us. Giving Christ the permission to dwell within us is the only way to prevent us from becoming self-lovers.

What do we naturally do? As a culturally impacted people, we strive for more information to find the answers and attend more conferences, seminars, camp meetings, committees, etc., believing that more information solves everything. As good as that can be, we rarely live up to the knowledge we have. Even Jesus said in John 5:39 that the scriptures don't have eternal life in and of themselves; rather they witness to who is the Eternal Life, Christ Himself. Some people idolize the Bible without idolizing the living word (Christ) of the bible. Information is not necessarily transformation. In addition, it is easier to know about God than to know God. It never fully becomes so experiential to have the impact that it can have. We are more informed 1,000 times over than the first-century church was, yet 2 Timothy 3:1-5 more closely defines our era than the era in which it was written. Paul says that possessing all the knowledge is worthless without agape love.[150] Would that mean that all the information we receive is worthless? Not necessarily, but it is worthless insofar as it may instruct us in how to look like Jesus rather than be like Jesus. Even learning about the Kingdom is not experiencing the Kingdom. Rather to experience the Kingdom I must allow God to come into me and then apply the promises of the Word by faith.[151] Everything we do, say, read, etc., should only be based on Christ living in us, actualizing our faith and transforming us into His image in *every* way.

However, only agape love is the true fruit and mark of a Christian. Living in this reality each moment diminishes our humanistic, self-living mindset. The kingdom is only revealed to the world as it sees Jesus act out the life of God in the flesh of his people. Becoming imitators of God is the kingdom of God activated within us.[152] Jesus said plainly that the kingdom is within, and when we know that, God's love is a dimension of all the information we receive. Therefore, to the degree that Christ lives in us, we live the kingdom. This is the foundation of the entire Bible. The essence of John 3:16 is found in

The essence of John 3:16 is found in all sixty-six books.

---

150. 1 Corinthians 13:2.
151. John 17:17.
152. Ephesians 5:1; Luke 17:20, 21.

all sixty-six books. It's also why Paul said that we could live in the love that was displayed on the cross, know God, and experience Christ. This is found throughout the parables, narratives, theology, and ethics of Jesus. In the end, it will produce a righteousness by faith that allows the foundations of God's love to radically impact all people. When Jesus is incorporated into every thought, breath, action, and impulse, then the love that surpasses understanding will be seen in the world as a bright light. The experience changes our focus from inward to outward. Though it will have its polarizing effect, nonetheless it will answer Satan's accusations against God, thereby solidifying the way, the truth, and the life in a people before the universe. By allowing this, we come under the dome of the King. The kingdom becomes a mighty tree that started from a mustard seed.[153]

Living in Christ is not an occasional experience, but rather a continual imbibing of His love towards us, regardless of whatever we may be thinking or experiencing at the time. It allows Christ to become real to us no matter what the situation may be so that we may be convicted of sin, righteousness and judgement,[154] and experience peace.[155] Therefore, if we have been declared righteous, we can have peace despite our circumstances, because our circumstances will always change. When we are aware of it each second of our lives, then we can ascribe the worth that God ascribes to us toward others. When this truth is superimposed over all things every moment, then we can see this truth spread horizontally toward others. We can recognize that God loves us no matter where we are in life, not searching for it, but realizing that he is near by faith. No matter our circumstances, God's love is multidirectional, not circumstantial, just as David experienced.[156] Paul also described in Romans 10:18-21 how God has always reached out to Israel and was always close to them.

Remember that love is the noun that God is, not just the verb that God does. When Paul said "we act, move, and have our existence in Him," we share in the body of Christ and allow the verb of love to become active and effective so that we become His hands, arms, and legs toward others. God always desires to pull us up to a higher experience with Him despite our feelings, circumstances, and situations. Romans 8:28 looks behind the circumstances and looks at the big picture that ultimately God wins, no matter what our poor decisions may have been. No matter what has happened to

---

153. Matthew 13:31, 32.
154. John 16:8.
155. Romans 5:1.
156. Psalm 139:8.

us, God fixes it. God can take the bad and turn it into good, if we allow Him.

Having the mind of Christ[157] is a promise upon which we can lean on throughout the day. In a concrete and real way, God's mind becomes part of us, thereby ascribing an unsurpassable worth to all of those around us. This is the mind of God, based on love, that allows us to become complete in Him to the point that we love our enemies. The promise is for those who walk in the Spirit moment by moment and pray without ceasing. Praying without ceasing is basically allowing your life to be an unbroken prayer. Therefore, ask God to give you the desire to plant the kingdom in your conscience all day long. If this does not happen, then we as the body of Christ are disconnected from the head of the body, which is Christ, and to the extent that this happens, we cannot and do not have His mind in us. In contrast, walking in the Spirit is walking with the mind of Christ. To be continually aware of the kingdom is having God's mind. Becoming "transformed by the renewing of our mind..." throughout the day and "tak[ing] captive every thought to the obedience of Christ"[158] is walking in the Spirit. When this daily experience takes place, we become what we think, and as Paul says, we *"are changed from glory (character) to glory."*[159] Giving God the permission to have His mind in us moment-by-moment allows us to see and do things that only God can do to reach others by using us, and to the extent that that happens, we are changed into His character. Therefore, when He returns *"we shall be like Him for we shall see Him as He is."*

As profoundly simple as it is, it's also profoundly challenging. Our minds become self-deceived, scattered, and forgetful. At the beginning of the day it's easy for our minds to focus on the future tasks of the day rather than focusing and living in the present. Also, our minds can easily rationalize experiences and opportunities away. The fact that we have not arrived at this point doesn't give us the right to judge ourselves. Judgment of ourselves blocks God's love as much as judgment toward others does; instead, we should move forward not taking it one day at a time, but one second at a time. Only when we are in the present do we realize that we live moment-by-moment. So therefore let us beware of each thought and awake each moment, not allowing the world to lull us into a life of mediocrity. Complacency is built upon the mundane, patterned errands and duties of life. Only by allowing God's mind and heart into us will we be more aware of others' needs around us. Take for example a clerk who checks you out at the

---

157. Philippians 2:5.
158. 2 Corinthians 10:4, 5.
159. 2 Corinthians 3:18.

grocery store. That person may see hundreds of people a day. The question is how can we show and ascribe God's love to that person and be different than others. Just telling her that you appreciate what she does can be a start. Ask God for the awareness of His thoughts each day and break the cycle of commonality.

Paul says, "be therefore imitators (followers) of God..."[160] The Greek word for "imitate" also means "shadow." My shadow does what I do; nothing more, nothing less. Shadowing God means to be like Him. To the extent that we live that way, we are living the kingdom of God within us. We are to live in love as Christ loved us and gave Himself for us.[161] The kingdom is found in this command. It's a dimension and depth we all should experience. Live in the command to love, receive, and give. The command to love others as God loved us is a holy act, which means that it is set apart from other acts. All characteristics and attributes stem from God's love, and this encompasses all other attributes of God. To live in love is continual, not just occasional, or when it's convenient. God's command to love should encompass all circumstances and situations in our lives, whether we have been wronged by others or we have wronged others. Jesus declares that His love is the same as the sun that shines on all people, the evil and the righteous, and as the rain that falls on the evil and the righteous.[162] That's how we should love. God's love doesn't discriminate or show favor. If our love is selective, then we are not living in love. It gives us the privilege to experience the mind of Christ, and this moment-by-moment infusion of God's love is only seen and given to those who desire God's love in their lives.

If our love is selective, then we are not living in love.

The extent to which I live...is the extent that I desire God's love to change me. I won't be defining who God is, but rather God will be redefining who He is to me. This is what Jesus said to Simon when he spoke of the prostitute woman: *"So I'm telling you that her sins, as many as they are, have been forgiven, and that is why she has shown such great love. But the one to whom little is forgiven loves little."*[163] This woman felt a greater need for a Savior than Simon did. Jesus has paid and given an unsurpassable worth to all, and ascribing worth to God should only be equal to ascribing

---

160. Ephesians 5:1.
161. Ephesians 5:2.
162. Matthew 5:45.
163. Luke 7:47.

worth to others. Whether they are friends, strangers, or enemies, we are still commanded to ascribe to them worth, just like God loved us. Simon and Matthew, both disciples, represent this. Even though Matthew was a tax collector and Simon a zealot, politically they represented the opposites of the first-century political world. Jesus never mentioned their political standings, but rather He unified them in love. Sometimes I believe He purposely brought opposites together just to show how His love unifies.

God's love is dynamic because the more we see it, the more we share it, the more we live it, and the more we are it. We can't live static lives where everything is always the same. Our lives are ever-changing and dynamic. Make each moment with your family a kingdom moment, and the same would go for co-workers, friends, acquaintances, etc. Ascribe worth toward others in godly ways. When meeting strangers, don't allow the curse of commonality to lull you into mediocrity. Our only task is to mimic God and act in love every moment through ascribing worth to all the people we meet. Let us do away with the tit-for-tat attitude and the pointing of fingers. Instead, let's bless others, bleed with others, and not fall back into the commonality and mediocrity of life. Even though we are, unfortunately, so conditioned to spiritual sleep, we can still battle the feelings of complacency through allowing Christ to spiritually awaken us.

Thought Questions on Kingdom Awareness

1) How do we stay spiritually conscious and awake for God?

2) Is it possible to be self-sacrificial? If so, how?

3) How does the world battle for our allegiance?

4) How does God's love counteract the influences of the world?

5) How do we unconsciously recreate God in our minds?

6) How do we, every second, tear down the strongholds in our life?

7) How does our judgment block God's love?

Kingdom Fearlessness

God is always at the center of the (King)dome, and by faith, we desire to be where God is. Only as we are living under the dome of the King can we experience the "peace that passes understanding."[164] Walking in peace is an attribute that God has given us through His righteousness, and through Christ, we can continue to walk in peace in His presence. Israel entered the earthly promised land. However, they missed entering the spiritual promised land. Hebrews 3:18-19 tells us that it was because of Israel's unbelief that they never entered the spiritual rest that God desired for them. Hebrews points out specifically that it was those who sinned against God that prevented Israel from their earthly entrance into the promised land. Their sin was a sin of unbelief against the promise that God, who led them out of Egypt, would make them into a kingdom of priests. They were unwilling to exchange Egypt for the promised land. Their heart was still secretly in Egypt, and they didn't want to let go of the experience they had in Egypt. Despite being slaves in Egypt, they focused on the food and comfort, even under the worst conditions. God desired something better for them, and at the same time, God would be magnificently revealed to the nations around them. It was God's plan that the Israelites would be the one nation of the true God, but instead, they became the proverb of

---

164. Philippians 4:7.

disgrace to the nations around them.[165] How is it with you? Do you truly want to be released from slavery, or does slavery provide some comfort for you? We all need the rest and peace from slavery in our lives.

Hebrews says the "rest" spoken of in chapters 3 and 4 was based upon a *better* resurrection, *better* country, *better* things, and *better* sacrifice.[166] Only those who truly desire to let go of Egypt will enter into the rest of Christ, but to let go is a faith experience. The good news is that we can still have that peace no matter what conflicts are in the news or in our personal lives regarding politics, war, financial issues, etc., because being under the dome of the King is not based upon circumstances or situations, for circumstances and situations will always change.

In the world, usually our circumstances define our disposition, and our lives change, but God doesn't. When our circumstances are dark, ugly, or discouraging, we must remember that God is beautiful, lovely, and faithful. Let's not allow our circumstances in life to define who we are, or who God is, but rather let us focus on God's goodness, despite our situations. Otherwise, if we allow our circumstances to define us, they will always appear larger than we are. When Nehemiah was discouraged, he was reminded that "the joy of the Lord is our strength."[167] The Hebrew word for "strength" is *maoz*, and it denotes "refuge." Also if you read Nehemiah 8:12, you will notice that the people were happy because they understood the law and character of God; therefore they had a feast and shared with the needy. They realized that their 'strength' and 'refuge' was the good news. The good news is based upon who Jesus is. Therefore, as with Nehemiah, let's not let our circumstances define us because God is larger than our problems are. Also, God isn't defined by circumstances or situations. Why? Because He already won the battle, and when He abides in us, we win, no matter what our circumstances are. His character doesn't change. He is sovereign, and His glory is forever and ever. When this, by faith, is realized, then our problems are small in comparison. Yes, it's true, in reality, it may be that our circumstance or situation may not immediately go away, but while we are in the midst of the problem, God is there, and we don't have to allow the problem to define us anymore. Kingdom living is living in this reality, a reality of faith.[168] Give Him the praise for that!

---

165. Deuteronomy 28:37.
166. Hebrews 9:23, 11:16, 11:35, 11:40, 12:24.
167. Nehemiah 8:10.
168. Hebrews 11:1.

Praising God is a form of spiritual warfare, as much as it is a form of worship. Even in the Old Testament, God prompted His people, under Jehoshaphat's rulership, to stand before the oncoming army of the Moabites and Ammonites and say, "Praise the Lord: for His mercy endures forever. ...and the Lord set ambushes against the children of Ammon and Moab."[169] Praise be to God for defeating the enemy! Literally! The forces of darkness desire for us to be defined by our circumstances, inciting fear, doubt, and discouragement. However, when we praise God ahead of time, we are reminded of who He is—His greatness, love, mercy, and sovereignty—and though we may have no idea how God will right the wrongs, remember the story of Jehoshaphat. Nothing is impossible for God because *His mercy endures forever.* To the extent that we give Him praise is the extent to which we are fortified for spiritual warfare. When we do this, it becomes a push-back against the forces of darkness that would otherwise consume our spirit. Therefore, amid our circumstances, choose to praise God. All of Psalm 136 describes God's mercy enduring forever despite the circumstances or situation of God's people. We are called to praise God all the time, just for the fact that He deserves it. Integrate the praise of God into your daily life and be thankful for all things. Not only does this free us up from doubt, discouragement, and fear, but also cynicism and negativity. As in Nehemiah's day, those who live under the dome of the King experience a different, separate, and unique relationship with God.

> *To the extent that we give Him praise is the extent to which we are fortified for spiritual warfare.*

Through our experience, we become witnesses and ambassadors for heaven and have our birthright changed from this earth to heaven's 'better' country. Also, we must remember our heavenly status supersedes any political opinions that we have on this earth. Therefore, as Paul wrote to Timothy, as a 'good soldier in Christ' we endure hardships on behalf of God and His name and we don't get "entangled with the affairs of this world." [170] Every day, we see more and more of the incongruences in this world's kingdoms compared to the heavenly kingdom. Most of the world doesn't desire to align itself with Jesus' kingdom because the sacrifice required is too high. God requires us to lay aside all presuppositions and fleshly desires and give Him the permission to change us into Jesus' image. God desires this both individually and collectively, and desires His

---

169. 2 Chronicles 20:21, 22.
170. 2 Timothy 2:3, 4.

body of believers to function and be unified in agape love. Our hope is not in trusting in people who have power over us, but rather trusting in God's love as a power under us and propelling us upward.[171]

Having spiritual courage and fearlessness is another characteristic of the kingdom. The level of anxiety in our world is peaking every day. Our culture has built-in daily fears. The counterpart to this is found in what Jesus said: "first be concerned about God's kingdom and His righteousness and all of these things will be provided for you as well."[172] As we live under the dome of the King and as Jesus drives out all of our fears, we can see that He destroyed the foundation for all fear, which is the fear of death: "Forasmuch then as the children are partakers of flesh and blood, he also himself likewise took part of the same; that through death he might destroy him that had the power of death, that is, the devil; And might free those who were slaves all their lives because they were terrified by death."[173] We can see in these verses that fear is slavery and the end of life supersedes all other fears. This verse shows that the reason why Jesus partook of our flesh and blood was for two reasons: 1) to destroy the devil that had the power of death and 2) to deliver those who always were under the fear of death. Therefore, God destroyed the underlying cause of fear—death.

Sigmund Freud spoke of ego defense mechanisms that are internal guards to protect against our fallen nature and deflect criticisms which are placed on us.[174] From our humanistic side, it feels natural for our fallen natures to defend self. Our nature is such that it projects criticism back out toward others, all for the subconscious reason that if we didn't, from a human perspective, it would lead to our demise. John said love dispels fear.[175] Matthew said, "Why, if God so clothes the grass of the field, which today is, and tomorrow is cast into the oven, shall he not much more cloth you, O you of little faith."[176] Many people walk around with the baggage of this underlying fear, and some are more sensitive about it than others. However, to live under the dome is to be unconcerned about common things, and rather to live completely without fear. Living under the dome is living under holy things. Remember the word "holy" is not a pretense for being better than anyone else but rather being separated for God's

---

171. John 12:32.
172. Matthew 6:33.
173. Hebrews 2:14, 15.
174. Sigmund Freud, Theories and Concepts, AROPA, 2013.
175. 1 John 4:18.
176. Matthew 6:30, AKJV.

purpose, as the Levites were— separated for a higher calling, from worldly things and humanistic reasoning such as Freud's ego defense mechanisms. This higher calling is to disseminate the character of God, ascribing worth to all with whom we come into contact. That is the higher calling, and that is the reason to be separate from the world. That which is common is common because everyone is doing it. It is the *zeitgeist* or spirit of the world. Wherever Satan develops this spirit, we can know that it becomes more common and universally accepted. How could the German people not see the devices and evils of Hitler and the Third Reich? Because if something becomes more universally accepted and evil becomes more hidden from people, then what is wrong may appear right and what is right may appear wrong. However, being under God's dome is being under the safety of Christ. Our "life is hidden with Christ in God"[177] Paul says this is what gives us correct discernment and peace. Furthermore, it helps us discern between light and darkness. And when we receive His life, we receive His power to stand when the world is under the *zeitgeist*. Therefore, when Jesus conquered death, it freed us also from the fear of death. The only truly healthy fear is to "fear God and give glory to Him…"[178]

Sometimes Satan uses many fears, and these become lodged in our fallen human natures, and our natures don't resist but rather comply with those fears, which may lead to a domino effect. For example, consider if we fear the loss of a job. It then leads to the fear that if we don't have money, we can't eat, pay rent, get fuel for our car, buy clothes, etc. Jesus tells us "…do not worry about your life, what you eat, or drink, or about your body what you will wear, isn't there more to life than food and more to the body than clothing? For the unconverted seek these things, and your heavenly Father knows that you need them. But above all seek His kingdom and righteousness first…"[179] It is a continual seeking and striving for the kingdom each day. The Greek word for "seek" in verse 33 implies "desire" (*zeteo*). In other words, we are to desire the kingdom, and if we lack the desire, we can ask God for it. He will even give us the desire for the kingdom. When Jesus spoke these words, it was to a people who had a lot less than most people have in our first-world cultures today. They were in abject poverty and under Roman oppression, and Jesus said 'don't worry about your life but rather seek the kingdom first.' What a radical thought and promise Christ made to those people and us! For them to

---

177. Colossians 3:3.
178. Revelation 14:7.
179. Matthew 6:25-33, NET.

step out in faith and refocus their lives on the kingdom is only possible with God. The primary thought that Jesus conveys is to live each moment desiring, striving for, and radically trusting God. Jesus says don't fear or worry about *"these things"* about which the Gentiles worry.

Paul says, "you did not receive the spirit of slavery leading again to fear, but you received the spirit of adoption, by whom we cry Abba Father. The Spirit Himself bears witness to our Spirit that we are God's children."[180] Fear manifests a spirit of slavery. To the extent that we are fearful, we are enslaved. Paul contrasts the spirit of slavery with the spirit of adoption, and when we know that we have the spirit of adoption then we can know that we can call our heavenly Father "Abba." We are no longer slaves to fear, "For God hath not given us the spirit of fear; but of power, and of love, and self-control."[181] God gives us a spirit that fears nothing, a spirit of courage, faith, hope, and peace. God spoke this to Joshua: "Be strong and of a good courage, fear not, nor be afraid of them: for the LORD thy God, he it is that doth go with thee; he will not fail thee, nor forsake thee."[182] Also, as previously mentioned, John says that "there is no fear in love because perfect love casts the fear out." [183]

Whatever our fear, God's love supersedes that fear. Therefore, to breathe every breath with the love of Christ is to live without fear, and the results of that prove that we are living under the King's dome by faith. To the extent that we live under the King's dome, it becomes to us a truly freeing experience. Most of the time, most of our fears are unrecognizable. Many people develop habits that are fear-based because of the underlying and foundational fear of death. The godly fear that should drive us should be rooted in who God is. As we stated earlier, if our God picture is not consistent with who He is as portrayed in His Word, then the drive of fear will be there. Or, if we know what His Word requires of us, and we don't act on His Word, we will become self-deceived, and then the unconscious fear of death will be an underlying motive within us.

> *We can't live in the abundant love of God while living in fear because they're mutually exclusive.*

We can't live in the abundant love of God while living in fear because they're mutually exclusive. There can be no real love, joy, and peace if we

---

180. Romans 8:15, 16 NET.
181. 2 Timothy 1:7.
182. Deuteronomy 31:6.
183. 1 John 4:18, NET.

are not living moment-by-moment under the dome of the King. The dome consists of the life of Christ and the eternal life based on Christ. John says, "And this is the testimony: God has given us eternal life, and this life is in his Son. The one who has the Son has this eternal life; the one who does not have the Son of God does not have this eternal life."[184] Being in Christ is having eternal life because only Christ's life is eternal. Eternal life is not necessarily a quantity of time, but rather a quality of life in knowing Christ. Not only is this the eternal life that John speaks of but it is the abundant life Christ spoke of as well.[185]

> *Eternal life is not necessarily a quantity of time, but rather a quality of life in knowing Christ.*

What prevents us from going in the direction of the abundant life? How does Satan dull and diminish the abundant life that Jesus gave us? Satan mainly works by lies because that's all he has—lies that produce fear. We buy into Satan's lies quite often. We think that we "need" this or that—ipads, movies, music, bad relationships, and many other unconventional and dysfunctional worldly desires. Not that some of these things are necessarily evil or bad in and of themselves, but so many people use them for self-centered living. They eat up time, and we become more self-absorbed in them. Plus, they may take our eyes off of kingdom living and ascribe more worth toward ourselves at the cost of others.

What Jesus said in Matthew 6 and His charge to not worry about earthly things is superseded by His promise to take care of our needs, and prompts us to focus on kingdom living. These earthly "things" contribute to the fear of bondage if we put them prior to seeking the kingdom first. When this happens, we recreate ourselves into something God never intended for us. We create it, fear it, live it, and then recreate God in our image, instead of allowing Him to create us in His image. We become more self-absorbed and, in reality, self-worshipers. We tend to redefine who God is based on worldly, external influences rather than allow the Word of God to define who He is.

In contrast, the abundant life has Christ alone as its source. Again, all worldly fears are based on lies, and that was the problem from the beginning. Satan changed Eve's picture of a beautiful God into a picture of a power-grabbing, egotistical, sadistic God. They bought into the lie, and that lie continues today. If you allow the world to change your picture

---

184. 1 John 5:11, 12, NET.
185. John 10:10.

of God, before you know it you will be worshipping yourself rather than the Creator. We read in Revelation 14:7 that *"fearing God"* is the healthy fear linked with the glorification of who He is, thereby revealing His character. Our source of life should not be the fears we live, but the glorification of who God is through us. The truth is that when we receive His life, He validates us in who we are in Him, thereby giving us no reason to create our own worth. The fact remains that God ascribes us worth and gives us his unsurpassable love that alone defines who we are and who we become. God's love that motivates and surrounds us gives us validation in Christ and carries a deeper validation and glorification of who God is toward the world.[186]

The kingdom paradox is that the more we cling to this world, the more likely we become like it and the more elusive His peace becomes. God desires to break all fear within us. "He that loses his life, for my sake, shall find it."[187] The greatest fear is that of death, and death is bondage to an unconscious behavior.[188] We may behave in certain ways unconsciously to avoid death. At the same time, fear is a self-fulfilling prophecy. In other words, we will behave in a certain way based upon our picture of God, and that picture is based upon what we think His character is like. The person who received one talent hid it in the ground because he feared the character of God.[189] His picture of God was distorted and thereby fear seized him and prompted him to behave in a way that was inconsistent with the real picture of God. The more fears a person has, the more one is in slavery to those fears. The more Christ is formed within a person, the freer they are and the more discerning of Satan's lies they become. Never allow the world or fear to dictate who you are in Christ. The true and abundant life only happens when all fear is given over to God. Our main priority is to reflect God's character of love to the world. "And walk in love, as Christ loved us and gave Himself up for us."[190]

---

186. 2 Corinthians 5:14, 15.
187. Matthew 10:39.
188. Hebrews 2:15.
189. Matthew 25:24, 25.
190. Ephesians 5:2, ESV.

Thought Questions on Kingdom Fearlessness

1) How do we enter God's rest?

2) Define spiritual courage?

3) How can we dispel Satan's fears in our lives?

4) What does it mean in 2 Corinthians 10:45 to bring captive every thought to obedience to Christ?

5) How does God's love supersede any fear in our lives?

6) What contrasts can we make in regards to our human picture of God versus God's picture of his Son?

7) In what way can we validate God's love in our lives?

The Single-minded Kingdom

The kingdom is based upon the high purpose of being single-minded toward Christ. James 1:6 states, "He who doubts is like a wave on a sea…" We previously spoke about this verse, but a wave is a metaphor for our lives. A wave doesn't have any independent existence; it doesn't determine where it wants to go; rather, it's just an extension of the motion that affects and surrounds it. It's moved and tossed by the winds around it, and when we are just living in the world each day, our lives become determined by our situations or circumstances around us, tossed this way and that way. When this occurs, we're not placing our lives under the dome of the King, and because of that, we don't receive much from kingdom life in God. Because of the aimless tossing in our mind, we're not having a strong foundation in the kingdom, but allowing our minds to be conformed to the pluralistic culture around us. And when we live our lives like a wave, our lives are only determined by our circumstances, tossed one way and another way, no determined direction or single mind. The Phillips version of Romans 12:2 says, "don't let the world squeeze you into its mold." In other words, don't become conformed to the world. Though we are pulled in two directions, only by putting Christ first can we resist the pull of the world. The word in Greek for "double-minded" is *dipsuchos*, literally "two-minded". Therefore, if we allow ourselves to be conformed to our culture, we will have two minds, and James says that when this happens, it creates *"instability."*[191] In other words, when we are in this condition, there is not one, consistent, stable mind that governs us throughout the circumstances and situations of our lives; rather, the circumstances and situations govern us and dictate our reaction to them, like a wave on the sea. Our call to the reality of the Christian walk is God's love toward us and our love towards others.[192] To the degree that we don't live in that reality we are double minded. To a certain extent the psychology behind situation ethics is centered around this concept. The mind would go in one direction based on the current situation, but when circumstances or situations change, it goes in another direction.

Throughout our day, we make these choices whether to stay within the mind of Christ or allow our circumstances to overcome our singlemindedness. James also says, "Submit yourselves therefore to God. Resist the devil, and he will flee from you. Come close to God, and He will come close to you. Cleanse your hands, you sinners; and purify your hearts, you double minded."[193] James is telling us two main thoughts. One, the word "submit" comes from the Greek *hupotasso*, which means "to place yourself under." In other words, we need to constantly be aware that we are in Christ, or under His domain, and desire to be there. Christ will give us the desire if we don't have it. Second, the word "resist" simply means "to stand firm in Christ." That's it. We don't have the power to fight the devil, and we are not even called to do so, but if we are constantly under Christ and stand firm throughout the day, then we can resist the devil.[194] Ultimately, James is saying that this is a way to cleanse our hearts and become single-minded. To the extent that we live with this single mind, God becomes our King and gives us refuge in His dome. If we react to our circumstances with a worldly mind, then we walk outside of His dome. To be single-minded is to be awake to God's calling, through the Spirit, every moment.

It's easy for the world to lull us into sleep and unfortunately we walk through life in a semi-conscious state. Our culture, daily habits, presuppositions, and preconceived ideas about the world have a certain grip that mesmerizes us. When this happens, we sometimes, if not often, become conformed to the world unaware. The contrast of being conformed versus being transformed is a moment-by-moment battle; we are either awake to

---

191. James 1:8.
192. 1 John 3:16.
193. James 4:7, 8, ISV.
194. James 4:7.

The Single-minded Kingdom

the world or awake to God. The good news is that we can have a transformed life every second of the day. The key is being aware of this throughout the day and staying awake to the Spirit. The earthly warfare requires us to stay awake in Christ each moment. This is the essence of Romans 12:2. As was previously mentioned, the Phillips version of this verse says, "don't let the world squeeze you into its mold..." Being conformed to this world unaware squeezes us into its mold. Therefore, the only solution against this zombie-like sleep is to be continually transformed (the Greek word is *metamorphoo,* from which we get the English word "metamorphous"). When a caterpillar changes into a butterfly, it's called the process of metamorphous. "Meta" means "with" and "abide" and "morphoo" means "transformed."[195] Therefore, we are transformed when we abide in Christ. This same word is used in Mark 9:2 and Matthew 17:2 for when Jesus was transfigured. Therefore, we are transformed by God, in Christ, through the Holy Spirit. We have no power to transform ourselves. It's God working inside of us. He does the transforming, and if we don't resist the transformation, we will have the fullness of who Christ is in our lives.

The moment-by-moment transformation is accomplished by having a new mind, a single mind, a kingdom mind. This happens on a continual basis, not just fifteen minutes in the morning. This is what Paul means by "walking in the Spirit" and "pray without ceasing." It is to have the presence of Christ within us all the time. If the mind wanders to where it shouldn't go, bring it back. Paul says God has given spiritual weapons, "mighty weapons through God, in order to pull down strongholds in our lives."[196] God's weapons cast down imaginations, obstacles, and false reasoning to the point where every thought is brought captive and obedient to Christ.[197] We come under God through submission and dependence upon His power and authority in our lives to battle against these spiritual forces. It's different from the world where people force others into submission by exercising worldly powers and authorities. Therefore, spiritual warfare is fought in our minds, casting down lies and bad thoughts and focusing on good and beautiful thoughts.[198]

The transformation of our minds enables us to determine what the will of God is for our lives. When this happens, we will have a clear and consistent directive of Jesus's will. The problem lies in the fact that our

---

195. Theological Dictionary of the New Testament, Abridged, Kittel, p. 607.
196. 2 Corinthians 10:4.
197. 2 Corinthians 10:5.
198. Philippians 4:8.

fallen human nature, or flesh, doesn't want this to happen, at least at first, but when we develop habits of continually allowing God to dwell within us, then the habit becomes formed, and we desire to glorify His character, ascribing worth toward God and others. However, Satan never gives up. We can never slide into the kingdom on auto pilot. Therefore, the first step of the battle lies within staying awake to the Spirit.

As we previously looked at the Greek word *perichoresis*, it probably is the most important word dealing with your relationship with Christ. Though the concept of mutual indwelling is found in the Bible, ironically the Greek word isn't, even though it describes the relationship of the Godhead. Nonetheless, God invites us to a relationship with Him, a mutual indwelling. It's the daily transformation (*metamorphous*) that takes place. Jesus said, "That they all may be one; as thou, Father, art in me, and I in thee, that they also may be one in us: that the world may believe that thou hast sent me. And the glory which thou gave me, I have given them: that they may one, even as we are one. I in them, and you in me, that they may be made perfected into one so that the world may know that you sent me, and you loved them as you loved me."[199] What a beautiful thought —God desires to unite us with Himself! As we are a purchased dwelling place, a temple of God, Christ desires to incarnate Himself into us. God Himself desires to walk in us and talk in us. That's what Paul means when he says, "in Him we live, move and exist."[200]

Because of this, God aspires to have us baptized into one body through His *perichoesis* (mutual indwelling). The church body is the bride of Christ. He is married to the church collectively, not as individuals. Otherwise, that would be polygamy. Therefore, all who make up the body of Christ is His bride. In the end, God's church will have a united function and goal. Collectively we become the body of Christ, revealing the character of God to the world through His unifying love. As much as God desires for an individual to be united with Him, when we align ourselves with the body (other members), we collectively become a huge picture of Jesus in the world. Then "the world is lightened (made to see) with His glory (character)."[201] God is put on display individually in us and collectively in His bride. Therefore, it will be said one day that "to know Christ is to know his body." The body is only functioning correctly as it listens to the head, which is Jesus. It's a similar analogy to when my arm or foot falls asleep. I

---

199. John 17:21-23.
200. Acts 17:28, NET.
201. Revelation 18:1.

can't use it properly; it's not functional. Therefore, if we individually as a body and the church as a whole fall asleep, we're not functioning properly. The body isn't awake to the head. Ninety-nine percent of the time, when we have a body, both individually and as a whole, that isn't listening to the head, we are involved in our own interests. When the body is awake to the head, then the head can direct the body where to go, here or there. Therefore, to the extent that we walk in the Spirit is the extent to which the body is connected to the head.

Being daily conscious and fully awake by walking in the Spirit, we ascribe worth to others, the same worth that God has ascribed to us. When we don't have this experience, our minds slip back into the world, and we become double-minded. Compared to the degree that we have this "walking in the Spirit" experience, we are single-minded and have allowed God's mind to permeate us on a continual basis. We need to see that only Christ in our mind can break the daily conformity of our mind to the world. Therefore, refuse to be conformed to the world and accept His transformation. Paul further says, "the worldly mind refuses to submit to the authority of God's Law because it is powerless to do so."[202] The worldly mind is largely formed by the patterns of the world and largely asleep to God's mind. Also, it has the pull of the world that resists itself against putting on God's mind. In contrast, a single mind desires the things of God against the pull of the world. If we don't transform into God's mind by *'walking in the Spirit,'* then these two minds battling for supremacy can produce a double-mindedness that inevitably leads to instability and self-deception.

The danger is when it is so subtle that we hardly feel and discern the pull of the world and drift further from the mind of Christ. Again, the battle lies within the mind. It's the battle between the mind of God and the mind of Satan. There is clearly no demilitarized zone. The habits we form daily are either for God or against Him, and many of the bad habits are formed almost imperceptibly. Our minds are never undecided or neutral, but the transforming mind of Christ wins, if by faith we allow God to work in us.[203] The fruit of the world's mind is anger, hatred, lust, envy, strife, and fear, whereas God's mind produces patience, love, compassion, faith, trust, hope, mercy, and grace. Staying awake in Christ and setting our minds on eternal, good, right, and holy things is the key.[204]

---

202. Romans 8:6, 7, ISV.
203. Romans 7:21-25.
204. Philippians 4:8.

We live in a dynamic, ever-changing world. Therefore, renewing our mind each moment is essential to kingdom living. Don't leave the kingdom mind only to be tossed by the waves of double-mindedness through doubt, fear, hopelessness, etc. Stay awake in the reality of the moment with the mind of Christ and push back against the evil thoughts of judging, anger, self-righteousness, hatred and any ugly thing that contrasts itself against the beautiful picture of God.

Let's break free from any cultural or societal thinking that has created any double-mindedness and stifled the mind of Christ. Integrating the reality of God's love towards us at all times will result in outreach to others and produce the fruits of Christ's mind in and through us. Straying from the kingdom mind defaults us into the worldly mind and instigates the instability of double-mindedness. Each moment we live can have eternal significance when we live with the mind of Christ.

> *Each moment we live can have eternal significance when we live with the mind of Christ.*

Ask God and allow Him to make you single-minded so that you can be *"filled with the fullness of Christ"* in the kingdom life, moment-by-moment.[205] Seeking the kingdom of God in every moment frees us not only from double-mindedness and self-deception but also from the slavery of sin and death. It frees us from judgment and assessment of others. Upon asking God for the power of His life and living daily with His new mind, we will see the inconsistencies in our lives more and more. We will then begin to see all the lies that we accepted from Satan. Through living under the dome, we will see the beautiful character of God in Christ and then common things will become holy. Remember, holiness doesn't make us more self-righteous, but when we become holy through Christ, we are separated for His high calling. Time will become more precious, and relationships will become more important. It will also expose anything in our mind that doesn't want to love and juxtaposes that against who we are and what we become. When God's agape love is blocked, we become more sensitized to the judgment of others, discontent with others, in conflict with others, etc. However, when these judgments are stifled through the Spirit, then the blocked flow of God's love is released, thereby creating worth toward others, at a cost to ourselves. God's love will become an outward love and antithetical to self-serving.

Christ in us has the authority to cast down judgments. I remember

---

205. Ephesians 3:19.

a time when I was at the airport in San Juan, Puerto Rico, waiting for a flight back to the U.S. As I was waiting to board, my mind started to slip away into assessing others. I started looking at people and assessing their behavior based upon who they were. Some parents were not doing a good job parenting, some had political t-shirts which I had disdained in my mind, one guy had no sleeves on his t-shirt, and I thought to myself, *what's he trying to prove?* I think to a certain degree our fallen nature desires these assessments. Then I assessed this one other guy by his sexuality or apparent gay lifestyle. As I boarded the plane, I found myself sitting next to him. We started to talk and had a great conversation. Then it hit me—when I was assessing or judging others, I was allowing Satan to block God's love and blessing toward others. By condemning them in my mind, I was thinking I was better than them, leading to my self-righteousness. Under these conditions, I asked myself, *How can God become glorified through me if, in my mind, I flirt with self-righteousness and ascribe more worth toward myself at the cost of others?* I needed to realign my mind in Christ, realizing He died for all and that we can love sinners and hate sin, just like Jesus exemplified throughout His life here on earth. Therefore, judgment of others blocks the flow of love toward others.

Another aspect of the single-minded kingdom is that we become "trees of righteousness the planting of the Lord, that He might be glorified."[206] As God moves in us through giving us His mind, the consistent growth allows us to respond to situations and circumstances as He would. We have a beautiful promise in that though we may fall during this process, God never leaves us or forsakes us, "the One who sanctifies and those who are being sanctified all have the same Father."[207] As someone once said, as long as the light is on, the darkness flees. Walking in the light is walking in freedom and liberty from sin.[208] Though the triggers of the world are still there to pull us in, as long as we are walking, moment-by-moment, in kingdom singlemindedness and kingdom love, the darkness is dispelled. Also, the more we behold God (that's a single-minded act), the more we become like Him.[209]

---

206. Isaiah 61:3.
207. Hebrews 2:11, ISV.
208. 1 John 1:7.
209. 2 Corinthians 3:18.

Thought Questions on the Single-minded Kingdom

1) What causes doubt in our mind?

2) What does it mean to be single-minded?

3) When we are daily transformed, what takes place?

4) What causes double-mindedness?

5) What does it mean to be "under Christ?"

The Kingdom of Abounding Grace

God came to give us His abundant life, and that life is only available when we give Him the permission to come into our lives daily. To the extent that we do this, moment-by-moment, He resides in us and His will becomes our will. Philippians 2:12–13 states that we need to "work out (katergazomai) our own salvation with fear and trembling/reverence." The Greek word *katergazomai* means "to overcome or accomplish."[210] Therefore, our salvation is Christ overcoming in us. It does not imply that it is my work or job to overcome, but more so to yield to Christ and the Spirit so that He, through me, overcomes. And Paul tells us why in verse 13: "For it is God that works (energeo) in you both to will and to do of His good pleasure." It is God's *energeo* ("energy" or "work") that leads us to do His will. It is God working in us that transmits the gospel. Mark 16:20 highlights an added element: "And they went forth, and preached everywhere, the Lord working (synergeo) with them, and confirming the word with signs following. Amen." The Greek word *synergeo* gave us the English word "synergy," denoting a team effort in which the whole is greater than the sum of the parts. When we allow Christ in us, then the *perichoresis* or "mutual indwelling" between God and us takes place. The same love that the Father and Son share is now available to us. This combination

---
210. Gerhard Kittel and Gerhard Friedrich. *Theological Dictionary of the New Testament* (Grand Rapids, MI: W. B. Eerdmans Publishing, 1986), 421.

produces the collaborative energy, power, and authority needed to accomplish Christ's purpose. The proof that we become transformed into His image is the proof that God is working in us to produce that reality.

From this, we then can love our enemies and have compassion on the less fortunate without judging them because we've allowed Christ inside us. This is also proof that being enabled, empowered, and motivated to love in a way that goes beyond the capability of our hearts. John says that *"we know that we have passed from death to life, because of our love, and the person who doesn't love remains spiritually dead."*[211] Love is the central sign of the kingdom, and when we manifest God's impartial agape love, people will be drawn to the kingdom through us. Living in the kingdom is replicating His life, both individually and collectively. The kingdom of God always displays Jesus and His self-sacrifice. To this degree, God is revealed to the world through us.

> *Love is the central sign of the kingdom, and when we manifest God's impartial agape love, people will be drawn to the kingdom through us.*

The church has missed the mark on its responsibility to exemplify the kingdom toward the world, be it our neighbors, friends, family or enemies. The sinner's prayer or a physical baptism does not magically transform a person, though sometimes we think it does. When you were baptized or conferred to Christ as a sinner, you made a pledge to Christ. The pledge to surrender your life is not the life itself you pledge to surrender. The actual life that you pledged to surrender is the life that you live after you make that pledge because the only life that we have to offer is the life of Christ in us, And we only have His life in us on a moment-by-moment basis. Again, the reason for this is because life is nothing but a series of moments strung together. Everything else is an abstract idea of what life is to be, but it is not life itself. Real life, which is the abundant life, is the life lived in Christ every moment. Marriage is like that. The vow we make to our future spouse to pledge our lives whether we are sick, poor, or dying is only as good as we live that pledge out in our lives moment by moment. Therefore, the pledge itself is not the life promised to the spouse, because the only life they have to give to each other is their present life.

The quality of our relationship with God is not based on the pledge I make to God, but on the relationship that I have with God that is based on the life of Christ in me that is lived out moment by moment. In other

---
211. 1 John 3:14, ISV.

words, I can pledge that I will die daily in Christ, but unless I allow myself through prayer and God's Word to die in Christ, verbally saying it means nothing. Therefore, a profession of faith is only that, a profession. If I just focused on having Christ live in me by faith moment by moment, then His desires become mine, His compassion becomes mine, and His love becomes mine. To the degree that Christ Himself lives in me moment by moment, those qualities will shine through me. Surrendering to Christ is the life we live moment by moment. Therefore, it is a continually surrendered life, and this is the daily spiritual battle. The question should not be *when did I surrender my life?* or *When was I baptized?* Instead, it should be *Did I surrender my life to Christ today?* Living the kingdom life is a string of surrendered moments to Christ. Paul says to see whether you are *'in the faith'* in 2 Corinthians 13, and this examining of our faith should also be throughout the day.

We will be known by our fruits whether Christ is in us moment by moment. Was I judging people today in my mind, based on their weight or if they smoke, etc.? To the extent that I'm aware of, Christ is in me and His character is being displayed to the world rather than elevating myself above others. We don't have to hammer it over our heads because we are not meeting up to the standard of Christ, but rather as a gentle reminder we can ask ourselves, *Did I represent Christ to my co-workers or boss today? Is Christ shining through me? Am I ascribing worth toward others as Christ has ascribed unconditional and unsurpassable worth to me? Did I collapse judgment of others?* We should ask the question based on Romans 6:3 "having been baptized into Jesus, I have been baptized into His death,"—have I died to self today?[212] Do I continually die to self moment by moment? A pledge becomes meaningless unless it is lived out daily. In addition a pledge may have good intentions but from a human perspective its not possible to keep. Only the promises of God toward us are the pledges that God keeps. Have faith in those. That may be the true reason why the living Christ is not seen in the church today. We mistake the pledge of life for the life we pledge. We think that because we promise to surrender our lives after we hear a great sermon or seminar that our life is a surrendered life. If we continue in that thought process, we become self-deceived. As James says, "be sure you live out the message and do not merely listen to it and so deceive yourselves."[213] Therefore, if we don't act on the truth, we become self-deceived in that we think we are living our pledge. Also, John says that if we don't incorporate the Word into our daily living, we

---

212. Galatians 2:20.
213. James 1:22, New English Testament.

won't live holy, separate lives, but rather common, worldly lives.[214] The holy life in Christ is only to be compared to that life which is unholy or common (of the world). Most Christians have a theoretical surrender and relationship to Christ. Therefore, most of their waking moments are devoid of Christ. We should ask ourselves the question, *Is Christ an integral part of my life today?* We may be "good" Christians, but being good and having God's goodness in your hearts can be different.[215] The lordship of Christ in our lives is only as real as it is lived moment by moment in our lives. The kingdom life is the 'real' life that Jesus said that was more "abundant" in John 10:10. And it's only real as we choose to make it real every moment in our lives. C. S. Lewis said that "…every time you make a choice you are turning the central part of you, the part of you that chooses, into something a little different from what it was before,…either into a heavenly creature or a hellish creature; either into a creature that is in harmony with God or else into one that is in a state of war and hatred with God….each of us at each moment is progressing to the one state or the other."[216] Therefore, if I don't resist the culture around me then my fallen nature is at default to absorb it. Our spiritual warfare starts in our minds.[217] Our choices decide our destiny and Jesus understood this well. That is why He said to "seek the kingdom first (the daily focus) and His righteousness and all of the other things will fall in place."[218] The question is, do our hearts seek the kingdom first? Living in the kingdom is taking every thought captive to Christ by seeking Christ first in all things. It's not a self focused purpose but rather a Christ centered purpose. In addition, we are not focused in on how well we are doing but rather how well Christ has done, otherwise we can become self-deceived. It's a simple and profound aspect, but it's missing in so many Christians today. We must be transformed by the kingdom rather than just know about the kingdom. Again, no matter how many books we read, seminars we attend, Bible studies we have. etc., unless they're applied to our daily lives, we will become self-deceived. The moment-by-moment experience is the true experience. Live in the now; the past is history, the future not yet, but the present is the only reality.

In Genesis 28:11-17, Jacob dreamed of the ladder with angels ascending and descending on it. In verses 16 and 17, Jacob said, "Surely the Lord was in this place and I didn't know it. And he was afraid (in awe) how holy is this place, it is the house of God and the doorway of heaven." For

---

214. John 17:3, 17.
215. Deuteronomy 28:49-58.
216. C.S. Lewis, *Mere Christianity* (New York, MacMillan Publishing, 1972), 86, 87.
217. 2 Corinthians 10:4, 5; 3:18; Proverbs 4:23.
218. Matthew 6:33, ISV.

Jacob, this was a reframing experience. Jacob saw this place in a different light, or as a picture with a different frame around it. Only afterward was he aware of the fact that God's presence was there in that place. This tells us that it's possible to be in God's presence and not even know it. It's also easy to see holy things as common. Even the church can forget the fact that we worship a holy Savior when millions upon millions of angels bow the knee, honor and praise Him constantly and consistently. Unfortunately, because of the daily, common life we live, its impact makes the church and everything around us common as well.

In Psalm 139, David had an experience in which God was near no matter where he was. He says, "You know when I sit down and when I get up; even from far away you understand my motives....you are aware of everything I do...Where can I go from your Spirit? or Where can I flee to escape your presence? If I were to ascend to heaven, you are there. If I make my bed in Sheol (hell), behold you are there... even the darkness doesn't hide from you"[219] Therefore, God is always moving in the hearts of people, in circumstances and situations, impressing people with holy experiences in their lives, but for most of us, like Jacob, we either don't recognize it or are unaware of it. God desires, by His grace, to make our common experiences that we have daily into holy experiences or holy encounters with others. Just as Jesus had encounters with the centurion or the widow of Nain, both found in Luke 7, we also can have encounters in our lives for a divine purpose. God's Holy Spirit is always striving with man to turn common experiences into holy experiences. In Acts 17, Paul explains the reason why God moves on the hearts of men. "He made from one every nation of men to dwell on all the surface of the earth, having determined appointed seasons and the boundaries of their dwellings. That they should seek God if perhaps they might reach out for Him and find Him, though he is not far from each one of us. For in Him we live, move about, and exist."[220] God is always active and dynamic in working for the salvation of each human being. The reason why God moves on the hearts of men is so that they can have His life. Unfortunately, most of the time, we are too spiritually asleep to notice His workings. He works in subtle ways, and those ways are only spiritually discerned. We frame our experiences as ordinary people living ordinary days with a list of chores to accomplish. However, as we go about our days, we should ever be aware that God's love surrounds us constantly. Are we aware of it? Are we aware of God's random acts of goodness towards us?

---

219. Psalm 139:2, 3, 7, 8, 12, NHEB.
220. Acts 17:26-29.

Do we bless others around us, or are we so focused on our daily task list that our spiritual walk is outside of us rather inside of us?

David said that God encompasses him always.[221] God's love surrounds us just like the air we breathe. The Hebrew word for God's love is *chesed*, which means "steadfast." God's love is an unwavering and steadfast love, not like human love, which rises and falls based on our circumstances and situations in life. God's love is a continual, surrounding, loyal love. Whether we are faithful or not, God's love continually surrounds us and never waivers. God is present in the ordinary, mundane, little issues of life, but He desires to make each encounter we have with others a holy experience, a glimpse of God to another person, and as much as we see God in them they will see God in us.

The other day I was at a park and noticed the children playing. Children value what we find ordinary. Simple things that would seem boring to adults are special to kids. Even watching little babies and their awareness of simple, little things is profound. A bird or dandelion to us is common, but to children, it becomes a new, deep experience, a wonder and marvel, a valued experience. We get conformed to worldly patterns as we grow up, and ordinarily, we think, *same old, same old, saw it before*. Our attitudes drown out the reality of things, and we replace it with conformity. Bills to pay, daily work, people that we are used to seeing each day, we live self-centered lives to meet our needs each day. We're often bored when wonders around us happen. We believe in God but mainly on a theoretical basis and our attitude is usually one of unbelief. Our entire existence is based on the now, but most of us think about the past and dream of the future. As we saw in Psalm 139, the world is full of God, but we frame it as ordinary, always looking for the next goal, a new car, to pay off the house, retirement, etc. We hypnotically buy into the common and ordinary way of doing life, which in the end only motivates us to live mediocre lives. It prevents us from experiencing God's kingdom. If we continue with this mindset, eventually we become blind to God's mercies.

We need to reframe our daily experiences because we are surrounded by God and angels, prompting us to see the holy instead of the common. When our frame of reference to the world always includes God, then we are under His dome. Stay awake to every spiritual opportunity, and ask God to make you aware of the opportunities to help others. Detach from the myopic experience of ordinary days. As you see different people each day, remember Jesus died for all of those people, which have infinite worth

---

221. Psalm 139:3.

The Kingdom of Abounding Grace

to God, and He desires to reach some of those through you, whether it be just making a positive remark about their job, encouraging them in some way, or even praying blessings upon them. Take life by living in the moment, and understand that each moment has an opportunity that you may never have again, whether it be telling your family, your spouse, your children, or coworkers that you care and love them.

Therefore, live your life in a kingdom manner and stay awake to heavenly realities. Too many times we live our faith in a fragmented and compartmentalized way. As James talks about double-mindedness, we must integrate our faith and become single-minded in our lives every minute. The next heartbeat of life is never promised to anyone. Grab the moment, see past the daily things of life and reframe them as opportunities to be fully awake to God. When we include the Lord in every present moment, we begin to align our minds with His mind and truth. Are the days you live kingdom-focused? Or are they lost in the world of cares and self-interests? Be always awake and develop the habit of putting on the kingdom mind. God is not ordinary. Therefore, we shouldn't frame our lives as if He was. We as kingdom people need to be awake and aware and ascribe worth to every human we encounter. Whether it is at a gas station, a checkout line, the bank, etc. Frame each encounter with others by ascribing them worth through interacting with them, because our small interactions could have a huge impact. I remembered seeing a sign that said, "To the world you are one person, but to one person you are the world." How profound! You never know how important our interactions could be to someone.

> *I remembered seeing a sign that said, "To the world you are one person, but to one person you are the world."*

Jesus exemplified these qualities. Here are several comments from the book *Desire of Ages* describing how Jesus ascribed worth toward the marginalized and downtrodden by coming under them.

> "He was possessed of one purpose; He lived to bless others."[222]
> "Jesus carried into his labor cheerfulness and tact."[223]
> "In every gentle and submissive way, Jesus tried to please those with whom He came into contact. Because He was so gentle and unobtrusive, the scribes and elders supposed that He would be easily

---
222. Ellen G. White, Desire of Ages (Mountain View, CA: Pacific Press) 70.
223. Ibid., p. 73.

influenced by their teachings."[224]

"*He often denied Himself of food in order to relieve those who appeared needier than He. He possessed a tact that none of them had or desired to have. When they (his brothers) spoke harshly to the poor degraded beings. Jesus sought out these very ones, and spoke to them words of encouragement. To those who were in need He would give a cup of cold water, and would quietly place His own meal in their hands. As He relieved their sufferings, the truths he taught were associated with His acts of mercy, and were thus riveted in their memory.*"[225]

"*He did not strive for worldly greatness, and even in the lowliest position he was content.*"[226]

"*Jesus did not contend for his rights. Often his work was made unnecessarily severe because He was willing and uncomplaining. Yet He did not fail nor become discouraged. He lived above these difficulties, as if in the light of God's countenance. He did not retaliate when roughly used, but bare insult patiently.*"[227]

"*He would not enter into controversy, yet His example was a constant lesson.*"[228]

"*He passed by no human being as worthless…*"[229]

"*Those whom he helped were convinced that here was one in whom they could trust with perfect confidence. He would not betray the secrets they poured into His sympathizing ear.*"[230]

"*Benevolence was the life of His soul.*"[231]

"*In his life no self-assertion mingled.*"[232]

"*So utterly was Christ emptied of self that He made no plans for Himself. He accepted God's plans for Him, and day by day the Father unfolded His plans.*"[233]

"*He was never elated by applause, nor dejected by censure or disappointment.*"[234]

"*He was never rude, never needlessly spoke a severe word, never*

---

224. Ibid., p. 85.
225. Ibid., p. 87.
226. Ibid., p. 88.
227. Ibid., p. 89.
228. Ibid., p. 89.
229. Ibid., p. 89.
230. Ibid., p. 92.
231. Ibid., p. 191.
232. Ibid., p. 260.
233. Ibid., p. 208.
234. Ibid., p. 330.

gave needless pain to a sensitive soul. Every soul was precious in his eyes. In all men he saw fallen souls whom it was his mission to save."[235]

"Though Christ had just been repulsed by the Samaritans, his love toward them was unchanged."[236]

"In all his intercourse with rude and violent men He did not use one unkind or discourteous expression."[237]

"He weeps with those who weeps and rejoices with those who rejoice."[238]

"In his contest with the rabbis, it was not Christ's purpose to humiliate His opponents. He was not glad to see them in a hard place."[239]

"He spoke no words of retaliation. He had a holy wrath against the prince of darkness; but he manifested no irritated temper."[240]

"Jesus alone could read his (Judas) secret. Yet he did not expose him. Jesus hungered for his soul."[241]

"Jesus spoke no word of condemnation. He looked pityingly upon Judas, and said, for this hour came I into the world."[242]

"change to "On Jesus's face he (Pilate) saw he saw no sign of guilt, no expression of fear, no boldness or defiance. He saw a man of calm and dignified bearing, whose countenance bore not

the marks of a criminal, but the signature of heaven."[243]

"Every feature expressed gentleness and resignation and the tenderest pity for the cruel foes. In his manner there was no cowardly weakness, but the strength and dignity of long-suffering."[244]

"From insult to renewed insult, from mockery to mockery, twice tortured by the scourge, all that night there had been scene after scene of a character to try the soul of man to the uttermost. Christ had not failed. He had spoken no word but that tended to glorify God. All through the disgraceful farce of a trial, He had borne himself with firmness and dignity."[245]

"Jesus revealed no qualities, and exercised no powers, that men

---

235. Ibid., p. 353.
236. Ibid., p. 488.
237. Ibid., p. 515.
238. Ibid., p. 533.
239. Ibid., p. 594.
240. Ibid., p. 619.
241. Ibid., p. 645.
242. Ibid., p. 722.
243. Ibid., p. 724.
244. Ibid., p. 735.
245. Ibid., p. 742.

may not have through faith in him. His perfect humanity is that which all his followers may possess, if they will be in subjection to God as He was."[246]

The above quotes further reveal that Jesus' character always embodied the spirit of divine love. He always ascribed an unsurpassable love toward all. In every situation and circumstance, He put on display that God is love. Therefore, put on Christ every day and allow the Spirit to impart His unconditional and unsurpassable love that supersedes any human reasoning within you. Let people see Jesus in you and you in Him. Jesus said, "...truly I tell you, inasmuch as you did it to one of the least of these my brothers, you did it to me."[247]

Allow yourself the daily habit of giving God the permission to change you through a deeper view of the life of Christ. We become incorporated into His life, and by living His life, He becomes revealed to the world.

However, don't be discouraged because it may take some time before this daily habit is formed. Judging yourself isn't any more productive than judging others. Stay awake in Christ every moment, and then you will find yourself under the dome of the King and God in you will be manifested to others.

> *Judging yourself isn't any more productive than judging others*

Thought Questions on the Kingdom of Abounding Grace

1) What does mutual indwelling mean?

2) How does the life that I live in Christ moment by moment put God on display toward others?

3) What is meant by the word "synergy"? How does it apply in your life?

4) What does it mean to be under the dome of the King?

5) How do we discern the difference between common and holy things?

6) How do we allow Christ to be an integral part of our daily lives?

7) What can we learn from Christ's life that connected Him to the needs of others?

---
246. Ibid., p. 664.
247. Matthew 25:40.

God's Kingdom Picture

The ultimate picture of Christ's love for us is Him dying on the cross for the whole world. Kingdom walking is based upon us internalizing this picture of Jesus. Walking in the kingdom allows us not to be defined by the circumstances around us, but by God's awareness, which then frames our lives into His life for us that day. It brings joy, peace, and love. It's a transformed life when we receive His new mind.[248] Walking in His love is based on the foundation that Christ loved us and gave Himself for us.[249]

Walking in His love is based on the foundation that Christ loved us and gave Himself for us.

Even though Jesus declared that He was *"the way, the truth and the life"* to His apostles in John 14:6, they didn't believe Him, especially when Philip asked *"if we can see the Father,"* Jesus said *"… you still don't know me? Why do you keep asking show us the Father?"* The apostles reasoned that the character of the Father was different from Jesus', and the purposes of the Father would be different as well. However, as Jesus stated, He is the revelation of the Father,[250] and that revelation is based upon God's love. It compels, surrounds, and urges us to not only see the Father but also reveal that same

---

248. Romans 12:2 and Philippians 2:5.
249. Ephesians 5:2.
250. John 14:9.

love of the Father to others. As a matter of fact, God's love is the main mark of unity to prove that Jesus' disciples are together as one. The love of Christ is Christ Himself, revealing the Father, and the love of Christ in us allows the Father to be revealed as well. The reason why Paul was motivated by God's love is that he was convinced that Jesus died for all, for all had unsurpassable worth. Paul saw people in terms of what God has done for them. That conviction compelled Paul and prompted him to live for others. When this happened, he ceased to be the center of his own world.

Paul saw God's love pulling him out of a self-centered pattern of life, and if we allow God to pull us out of that same pattern of life, we will enter the life of Christ. Jesus said when we lose the self-centered life, we find our real and true life, which is God's life in Christ, the abundant life.[251] Jesus knew that His life within people would make them live for others. This is what Paul experienced.[252] Isaiah clearly says it's a life of selfless living. God saw that Israel's worship centered around themselves and how good they looked. "They seek me day after day and are eager to know my ways …they are eager to draw near to God. 'Why have we fasted,' they ask, 'but you don't see' 'Why have we humbled ourselves, but you don't take notice?' Look! You on your fast day you serve your own interests and oppress all your workers. Look you fast only for quarreling, and for fighting… You cannot fast as you do today and have your voice heard on high. Is this the fast that I have chosen, merely a day for a person to humble himself and bow down one's head like a bulrush, for lying on sackcloth and ashes? Isn't this the fast that I have chosen: to loose the bonds of injustice and to untie the cords of the yoke, and to let the oppressed go free, and to break every yoke. Isn't it to share your bread with the hungry, and to bring the homeless poor into your house; when you see the naked, to cover them with clothing… Then, your light shall break forth as the dawn and your healing will spring up quickly; and your vindication will go before you, and the glory of the LORD will guard your back. Then you'll call and the LORD will answer… if you do away with the yoke among you, and pointing fingers and malicious talk. If you pour yourself out for the hungry and satisfy the needs of afflicted souls, then your light will rise in darkness… And the Lord will continually guide you."[253]

We can see Israel's attitude of worship was a self-seeking one, but when all forms of self-seeking and self-living are given over to God, including

---

251. John 10:10.
252. 2 Corinthians 5:14, 15.
253. Isaiah 58:2-11, ISV.

judging and pointing our fingers at others, then God's light will shine forth in our lives. It also brings healing to us. Having a form of worship does not mean that there is a power that accompanies it. The character of the righteousness of God will be revealed when we call on the Lord, and He will hear us, and His light will arise out of darkness, and the Lord will continually guide us. When self is removed, a powerful conviction from the Holy Spirit occurs, bringing holiness and glory, and the character of the Lord is revealed. The question is not that we believe this, because most people may believe it, but rather are we convicted by it. This conviction will bring to action our faith, and we become "doers of the word and not hearers only, deceiving ourselves."[254]

Does your nature desire to live in this conviction and be impacted by it? Will you allow God to change the directions of your ingrained life patterns? Belief and conviction, in our age, are two different words. In other words, are we convicted of it when we need something or something is broken in our lives, and we know we must fix it? If we prepare food to eat, we are convicted by the fact that we are hungry. If I fix a broken window, I'm convicted by the fact that if I don't fix it will either let cold or hot air in the house. Many people who profess Christianity may not testify to the fact that they are convicted by it.

Therefore, the paradigm shift is in the fact that we may not be living *the* life, but rather *my* life. My God view may need to be totally changed or tweaked a bit more. Only Christ in me can fix it. Not me and a little help from God, but rather 100% of God in me, as Paul said, *"Christ in you, the hope of glory."*[255] We must come to the point where we recognize that we can't fix it. After all, when our will is given over to Christ as 1 Thessalonians 5:24 says, then *"faithful is he who called you who will also DO IT."* God's faithfulness doesn't rest upon me, but rather it is His faithfulness in me that will accomplish His desires in and for me so that He receives the glory. However, I need to submit my will to God for this to happen. We still need to be convicted, whether things are going well or going badly. If we lose our job, are we still convicted? When we have financial problems, are we still convicted? When the doctor says we have six months to live, or when our child has terminal cancer do we still believe that "all things are working together for good?"[256] In other words, are we as convicted of God's truth as we are that the sun will rise tomorrow? Having the love that

---

254. James 1:22.
255. Colossians 1:27.
256. Romans 8:28, ISV.

compels us brings us into the single mind of Christ. Our situations in life may change, but we need to be convicted that God's love toward us does not change. The question we need to ask is, *Are there areas of our lives that have a conflicting picture of God?* In a book called *The God Shaped Brain*, our picture of God can have a determining physiological effect on how we change, "when we worship a god other than one of love,---a being who is punitive, authoritarian, critical or distant, fear circuits are activated and, if not calmed, will result in chronic inflammation and damage to both brain and body. As we bow before authoritarian gods, our characters are slowly to be changed to be less like Jesus. ...But worshipping a God of Love actually stimulates the brain to heal and grow. Truly, by beholding we are changed, not only in character, but our neural circuitry as well."[257] Ask God if there is anything that is blocking the altogether beautiful picture of God and have it brought forth to be removed. It may be subconscious or repressed. We receive a lot of wrong ideas and concepts about God every day from the media, friends, family, etc., and we don't even realize the impact they may have on our God picture. Therefore, if we don't spend time incorporating God in us through prayer and His Word to clarify who the real God is, then inevitably our picture of God will be changed by our culture around us. Even Scripture verses can be strung together to form an arbitrary picture of God.

The first-century Jews saw God as an exacting God that required an absolute obedience to His law and even made up a few hundred human laws.[258] They replaced their picture of God as a merciful, loving, compassionate God, described in Exodus 32 with an arbitrary and vengeful God. This incongruent picture of God became so strong in their belief that when Jesus arrived on the scene, it stood against everything they thought was true. Their picture of God was one that required strict and exact obedience to every detail of the law. However, Jesus said He came to *"fulfill"* the law. The Greek word for "fulfill" is *pleroo*, meaning to "fill full." The law went deeper than most realized and Jesus was going to fill the law full of meaning. It could be said that Jesus came to fill the law full of Love. In other words, the law went deeper from just an outward appearance of those who keep it. Jesus said if a brother has anger against another brother, he has committed murder already in his heart.[259] Therefore, our picture of God is also formed through the deeper spiritual meaning of the law.

---

257. Jennings Timothy, *The God-Shaped Brain*, 27.
258. The Mishna was formulated in the third century B.C. defining many ritualistic laws.
259. Matthew 5:21-23.

The Jewish religion replaced a love-filled picture of God with a stoic and arbitrary picture of God that had vengeful consequences for anyone who would stand against it, whether it be a Roman or Jesus Himself. Job battled the incongruent picture of God that developed in his mind through suffering and not understanding why he suffered. Even friends and family have worldviews that are usually molded by society and culture that run inconsistent with a true biblical picture of God. All of this information can have an impact on what we expect from God and how we believe we should respond to God based upon particular situations in our lives. It's hard to be motivated by God when our picture of God is distorted in any way. Many times, we believe what is true, only to find out that we were never truly convicted by it, especially by God's Word. Only through spending time in God's Word and prayer can we understand all of Christ's loving attributes and what He has done for us, bringing us into a correct perspective of a God who desires the best for us, and teaching us how we can then integrate that picture of God toward others. Just one verse can have this impact; however, put other verses together, and a beautiful picture of God emerges. For instance, I recently found something special in Hebrews 13:15. It's a verse that I have read many times before, but as it stands out by itself, it drives home a concept that is simple and powerful. It says, "Through Him, then let us continually offer up a sacrifice of praise to God, that is, the fruit of our lips, acknowledging His name." This verse opened to my eyes that our reasonable daily and continual sacrifice should be to praise Him continually no matter how bad a day I had or how emotional I feel that day. It shouldn't matter what the circumstances are in my life because He deserves worship no matter what. He deserves worship continually because His death reveals the fact that a God of love dies for His enemies[260] of which opens up His beautiful life.[261] God is sovereign despite what's going on in my life at that time. Therefore, my picture of God shouldn't be based on my circumstances or situations. God's love leads us to repentance, as Romans 2:4 says. Therefore, we can't even take credit for our repentance.

The purpose of God releasing judgment against us was to free us

> *The Greek word for "fulfill" is* **pleroo,** *meaning to "fill full." The law went deeper than most realized and Jesus was going to fill the law full of meaning.*

---

260. See Romans 5:6-10.
261. 2 Corinthians 5:14, 15, 21.

from the bondage of sin and death.²⁶² It was "for freedom that Christ set us free."²⁶³ The bondage of fear is only broken when we can see Christ's insurmountable love for us and His desire to set us free from the bondage of sin. The beauty is that God's love meets us in our fears, anger, lust, hatred, discouragement, hopelessness, etc. Hebrews 2:11 says that "he who sanctifies and they who are being sanctified are one." Christ set us free by His life so that we receive His freeing life, a life free from self.

Does our personal conviction of God's love for us have the power to change us from a mindset of guilt, shame, threats, and fear? Anything less than a comprehensive appreciation of God's sovereign love, in and through us, will ultimately lead us to a subconscious rebellion against Him. Job didn't know about God's encounter with Satan before Satan tested Job. Job subconsciously felt that it was God attacking him.²⁶⁴ Job came close to rebellion against God, yet God said to Job's friends *"you haven't spoken correctly about me, as did my servant Job."*²⁶⁵ Only God's love in and through us can make us truly obey Him. The Exodus taught us that the obedience that springs forth from fear would only be temporary and in the end, form the character of a rebel, because deep down inside our fearful hearts, we are not truly wanting restoration.

Our picture of God directs the love motive in our hearts and only to the degree we grasp more of God's love can we love more. That is why Satan directly attacked God's character in Genesis 3 and distorted the picture of God for Eve for her to rebel against God. Satan's tactics were nothing but a bunch of lies. These lies were the same that Lucifer pawned off on the fallen angels. Satan's deceptive manipulation is called "traffick" (Hebrew *rekullah*), and it means "merchandising" and "trading."²⁶⁶ Not only did Satan do this to himself, but he did this to bring down one-third of the angels in heaven.²⁶⁷ This word "traffick" is trading and exchanging the truth about God for a lie. After Satan and the angels had fallen from truth, Satan desired all of mankind to buy into the same lie. The same lie has its foundation in questioning the character of God within His law. Again, "traffick" is defined as exchanging any truths about God for lies.

In Genesis 3:4, Satan's first lie was "you won't surely die." The second lie was in verse 5: "you will be like God," and the third was in verse 6: "the

---

262. See John 5:24.
263. Galatians 5:1, NET.
264. Job 9:22-24; 10:8; 10:16, 20; 21:17-26; 30-32; 24:1-12.
265. Job 42:7, ISV.
266. See Ezekiel 28:16, 18.
267. Revelation 12:4.

tree was desired to make one wise." The "trade" or "exchange" that Satan was making was that of a beautiful picture of God for a self-centered, power-hungry, egotistical picture of God. Instead of seeing a loving creator God, with Adam and Eve's best interest at heart, Satan corrupted Eve's thoughts by exchanging a trust of God they had for a doubt about God and ultimately Eve believed it. Eve bought the lie and felt that God was perhaps threatened by them and didn't have her and Adam's best interest at heart. Satan created this ugly picture of God to get a disobedient response from Eve—eating the fruit of the forbidden tree. Satan backed Eve into a corner by having her believe lies about God. Therefore, to her, it appeared that her only option was to eat the forbidden fruit. Also, referring to the fruit on the tree, Eve misquotes God by saying "you must not touch it lest you die." God never said that and Ellen White states, "This statement of Eve gave him (Satan) the advantage; he plucked the fruit and put it in her hand using her own words...You see no harm comes to you from touching the fruit neither will you receive any harm by eating it."[268] Once she had the correct picture of God, she should never have allowed Satan to change it, or 'traffick' (exchange) it into a lie. Eve had the opportunity, as does every Christian, to incorporate the correct picture of a loving God.

Paul said, "for the weapons of our warfare are not of the flesh, but divinely powerful for the destruction of fortresses. We are destroying speculations and every lofty thing raised up against the knowledge of God, and we are taking every thought captive to the obedience of Christ."[269] Therefore, since Eve did not "cast down the thoughts" because they were the wrong view of God, Satan's views of God replaced her correct view, usurping the knowledge of the authority of God and Satan's authority took God's place through reasoning. The word in Greek for "imaginations" is *logismos,* and it means "hostile reasoning." "It is reason in its concrete form in the consciousness and worked out in action."[270] It pertains to the way we reason and think. Paul says that when a man rejects God, he becomes "futile" (*mataio*, which means "empty") in his thinking or *Diaglogismos* ("inward reasoning").[271] Through God's power, we're commanded to 'cast off' these false 'hostile reasonings' and lies. Paul further says in Romans 14:1, "Receive anyone who is weak in the faith, but not for doubtful (Dialogismos = inward reasoning), disputations (Diakrisis = discerning)."

---
268. Ellen White, *Confrontation* (Washington DC: Review & Herald Publishing, 1971), 14.
269. 2 Corinthians 10:4, 5, NASB.
270. Gerhard Kittel and Gerhard Friedrich, *Theological Dictionary of the New Testament Abridged in One Volume* (Grand Rapids, MI: W.B. Eerdmans Publishing, 1986), 536.
271. Romans 1:21.

In other words, a lack of faith contributes to one's reasoning becoming clouded and undiscerning. Paul further says, "Do all things without murmuring and disputings (Dialogismostion = inward reasoning)."[272] Therefore, we can see that because Eve didn't "cast down" and "bring into captivity" the truth about God, the false picture that Satan created was feeding her and she succumbed to the lie and the battle in her mind was lost at this point. The sad part is that ever since the fall in the garden a long time ago, mankind has still been buying into that lie and eating from the forbidden tree. Trying to find life from other things beside the God of love, such as media, partying, substance abuse, etc., only creates a spiritual void in one's life. Therefore, exchanging the truth of Christ for anything else in this world is buying into Satan's lie. In reality, without God, we are all dead people walking. All sin can be linked to the idea of buying into lies to become our own gods through self-recognition, a desire to be noticed, materialism, seeking a fortune, etc.

In reality, without God, we are all dead people walking.

Therefore, we must correct our picture of God, and the best place to start is in John 14:9: "if you have seen me you have seen the Father (God)." For centuries God's prophets directed Israel and Judah to an accurate picture of God, but now in these last days, God's picture has been definitive in Christ.[273] Focusing our all on Jesus not only reveals God to us but also changes us into His image (character).[274] Jesus became the Anointed one spoken of in Isaiah 61:1-3 for the purpose of anointing His priesthood for their work of putting God on display. Speaking of this, Isaiah says, "The spirit of the Lord GOD is upon me; because the LORD hath anointed me to preach good tidings unto the meek; he hath sent me to bind up the brokenhearted, to proclaim liberty to the captives, and the opening of the prison to them that are bound; To proclaim the acceptable year of the LORD, and the day of vengeance of our God; to comfort all that mourn; To appoint unto them that mourn in Zion, to give unto them beauty for ashes, the oil of joy for mourning, the garment of praise for the spirit of heaviness; that they might be called trees of righteousness, the planting of the LORD, that he might be glorified." Jesus was anointed to set the captives (the whole world) free from the bondage of sin and lies. Whatever healing you need, Jesus has it. The purpose of the healing is to

---

272. Philippians 2:14.
273. Hebrews 1:1-3.
274. 2 Corinthians 3:18.

be as a planted tree of righteousness so that He might be glorified. Hebrews 1:3 says that Jesus is the "express image" as the Father. Here the Greek word *karacter* is used only once in the whole New Testament. Therefore, Jesus is the same character of the Father. When Moses wanted to see the glory or character of the Lord in Exodus 33:19, God said that He would "proclaim" the name of the Lord, so in Exodus 34:6, 7, He said, "the LORD, the LORD God, compassionate and gracious, slow to anger, and filled with gracious love and truth. Having mercy on thousands forgiving iniquity, transgression and sin; He doesn't leave the guilty unpunished, responding to the transgressions of the Fathers upon the children and the children's children until the third and fourth generation." It's a beautiful thought that God has mercy on thousands. Therefore, proclaiming the name of the Lord is proclaiming the beautiful character of the Lord.

Truly we can say that the glory of God shines in the face of Jesus Christ.[275] Reframe your picture of Jesus in the light of His bondage-breaking power. Jesus said in John 17 that His desire was to be within us. Immerse yourself in the Word, for it's the only way to be set apart for His holy service and healed at the same time. Spend time each day reflecting on what Christ has done for you. Being fully convicted of the true picture of God will set forth the direction God wants for your life. Until we are fully convicted of that, we cannot become fully compelled.

> *Reframe your picture of Jesus in the light of His bondage-breaking power.*

Furthermore, make sure that you develop the habit and carve out time for God. David, Moses, and others felt that the morning was the best time to start.[276] To the degree that I forget to, or intentionally don't do His will, is the degree to which I drift back into the world. I will become more secularized and have a worldlier mindset. My capacity to forgive and love will become more diminished each day, and all the attributes that I desired in Christ will drift into the world. The saddest part is that I may not even know it's happening.

---

275. 2 Corinthians 4:6.
276. Psalm 5:3; 59:16; 88:13; 90:14; 143:8.

Thought Questions on God's Kingdom Picture

1) What did Paul personally experience to live for others?

2) How can you have the same experience Paul did?

3) What is the difference between being convicted versus being convinced?

4) How can people change their picture of a merciful God to one of a vengeful God without even knowing it?

5) How can we distort our picture of God?

6) What happens when we praise God continually?

7) How did Satan change the truth of who God is into a lie to Eve?

Kingdom Centeredness

The main obstacle that prevents us from entering the center of the kingdom is self. In Luke 9 Jesus said, "If anyone desires to come after me, let them deny himself take up his cross daily, and follow me." The hardest part of this statement is denying ourselves. As a matter of fact, our hearts are so deceptive that when we think we are denying ourselves, we might not actually be denying ourselves. True self denial is allowing Christ in us so fully that His will becomes ours. Thereby it's not focused on me, but rather it is an outward denying for others' sake. It is allowing God to come into our lives and fellowship with us so much that we identify with God's natural impulses to reveal His life in us. It is "Christ in you the hope of glory."[277] We may have some examples of dying to ourselves, but the true denial of self, which can only come through the Spirit, is living for God and others, because those who "save their life (not denying themselves) will lose it but those who lose their life for my sake (Jesus lived for others) will "find (save) it."[278]

The whole process of the Christian life is learning how to die that we can truly live. We don't have to focus on behavior, but rather on the life of Christ, and remain in Him throughout our day; then our behavior will conform to Jesus' life. As we said earlier to live more abundantly, we must

---

277. Colossians 1:27.
278. Matthew 10:39.

enter and remain under the dome of the King. The "kingdom of God," Jesus said, "is within,"[279] and how much Jesus is within us will determine how much we are in the kingdom. Not that we could actually have one foot out and one foot in, but unfortunately many people live their lives in a double-minded way. When we incorporate Jesus in us by giving Him the permission to come inside us each day, we then will notice more and more the small voice of God that guides us where to go, who to see, and what to say. The kingdom represents the domain of the King we serve. Therefore, when our lives come under the dome, which is Jesus, then we are living under God's domain and not Satan's. It's important to remember that we accept Christ's invitation to be part of His life, being in the center of His life.

Jesus said, "I pray not that you take them from the world, but that you keep them from the evil one."[280] The Greek word for "keep" is *tereo* and it means "to guard and protect," or "shield" them. In other words, when we are shielded by Christ we are under His domain, and unless we take ourselves out of the King's domain, we remain in Christ. When we are in Christ, we can have faith that whatever happens in our lives is for our best interest and God's glory. God's best interest is to reveal Himself through us in the Spirit.[281] Being under God's domain is also the shielding spoken of in passages such as, "I will hold you with the right arm of my righteousness…"[282] The fact that God is holding our hand further defines us as living under the domain of the King. Therefore, no matter what our situations or circumstances are, when we live under God's domain, we live under His will. It doesn't mean that there is no suffering. Peter echoes this as a part of spiritual restoration. "After you suffered awhile, the God of all grace who called you into His eternal glory will restore you, establish you and strengthen you, and support you."[283]

We saw that the word for 'kingdom' in Greek is *basileia* and it means "dome." That is why some churches are called basilicas because they are domed churches. The church *(ecclesia)* is "called out" from the world. In ancient times the people would go into the *basileia* and it was used as a metaphor for a church. Hagia Sophia, one of the oldest and largest churches within Christianity in Istanbul, is based on this dome concept. However, to get to the dome of the King, we must take up our cross and

---

279. Luke 17:21. Some versions have the word "midst" in Luke 17:21 referring to Jesus as the kingdom within their midst. Either way, Jesus still refers to Himself as the kingdom.
280. John 17:15, WEB.
281. John 16:7.
282. Isaiah 41:10.
283. 1 Peter 5:10, ISV.

deny ourselves. To the extent that I give self up and take up the cross is the extent to which I come under God's kingdom of selfless living, but it is only Christ in me that can enable me to live a selfless life. Therefore, to be "called out" from the world is to deny self and by denying oneself and receiving Christ's victorious life we come under the dome of the King. How do we get to the center of the dome?

Let's look at a merry-go-round as a metaphor. A merry-go-round in a school yard works in the way that the closer we get to the center the less spin there is, and the farther from the center, the more centrifugal force, and the harder it is to hold on. As Christians, we need to get to the center because the pull of the world on the edges of our lives forces us to get off the merry-go-round and then it becomes harder to get back to the center. The deception that we looked at in James is that many may think that they are in the center of the dome, but in actuality, they may be just at the edge of the merry-go-round of life. Paul alludes to this in the letter he wrote to Timothy, they will hold to an outward form of godliness but deny its power.[284] When we're connected to Christ, the circumstances and situations of life pull us toward the edge. It could be mental, physical, emotional, material, work, or just life in general. Many of these things can be good things, but they can still pull us away from the center of the kingdom, just as in the parable of the seed where Jesus said, "the cares of this world choke out the seed."[285]

Paul brings this all into one category called, "the works of the flesh."[286] These can sometimes clothe themselves in apparently good things that we think of and do throughout the day, but they are still laced with self. There's nothing necessarily wrong with certain things in life, except for the fact that they can replace God in the rat race of life. Anything outside the dome is a flesh existence. It's a false way of life, clothed as true. Again, we may believe the truth, but if we don't live the truth we become self-deceived.[287] Anything outside the dome is irrelevant in the big picture.

The oxymoron is that when we deny ourselves, we find a new life in Christ. When we become part of the world, the world starts to own us, but while under the dome of the King, the world can't touch us because of our death to it. We will never say "I've arrived" because we are not focused on our performance. Our focus is not on us, but rather on being in Christ. Paul says "Keep examining yourselves whether you are continuing in the

---

284. 2 Timothy 3:5, ISV.
285. Matthew 13:22.
286. Galatians 5:19-21.
287. James 1:22.

faith,"[288] which relates to the question, *Am I revealing Christ?* If not, then I must examine if I am in Christ. The Spirit always brings to us a checks and balances system. The Spirit never convinces us that by doing "good things" we can merit our standing with Christ. It's related to what Jesus spoke of in Matthew 25 when the supposed righteous recalled all the great things that they did while the actual righteous did not remember any righteous acts they did.[289]

The truth sets us free from everything that enslaves us, and when we surrender everything, whatever has held us in bondage no longer owns us. Therefore, when people try to take things from us, we have already given them up in our minds. Living in the center of the dome is a daily, moment-by-moment decision to allow Christ to abide and dwell within us daily.[290] We are only alive to Christ as we are dead to self.

> *We are only alive to Christ as we are dead to self.*

During Christ's life, and more generally in first-century Roman times, many different societal issues were brewing on several levels. However, Jesus was trying to redefine what the kingdom was to all classes of people, including the Romans. The characteristics of the kingdom that were on display through Jesus's life were those that all could have through Him. Jesus clearly presented a kingdom that was different from any other worldly kingdom, and He was showing and describing the differences. With that in mind, it was a kingdom that Jesus promoted as attainable through Him.

What Jesus was putting on display was the Father living in and through Him. Challenging enough was the need of Jesus to correctly define the kingdom to his apostles, but even more so to redefine it for many Jewish factions that existed at that time. This display of who God is was a paradigm shift for most people during Jesus' time. In Luke 17:20, 21 Jesus says, "And when he was demanded of the Pharisees, when the kingdom of God should come, he answered them and said, the kingdom of God cometh not with observation: Neither shall they say, lo here! or, lo there! for, behold, the kingdom of God is within you." The words "cometh not with observation" denote that nothing of the kingdom is perceptible through the senses. However, let's look at some of the Jewish factions that challenged Jesus through their definitions of what they thought the kingdom was.

---

288. 2 Corinthians 13:5, ISV.
289. Matthew 25:31-46; 7:21-23.
290. See the parable of the vine in John 15.

THE PHARISEES: The first-century Pharisaic Jews were legalistic in the sense that if they could fix the Jewish masses through manmade regulations of Jewish customs, then God would honor them and release the Jewish nation from Roman oppression, thereby reestablishing Israel as a sovereign kingdom that would rule the world.

THE SADDUCEES: The Sadducees maintained the temple and were even more politically connected to the Roman government than the Pharisees were. They shared many beliefs with the Pharisees but felt that if they could connect politically to the Romans in such a way that they would release Israel from their rule, then they could become an independent nation once again.

THE ZEALOTS: The Zealots believed that if they could get enough Jewish people to believe in their ideology and the mighty intervention of their "warrior" God, then they could rule over the Romans by force and set up God's kingdom on His behalf.

THE ESSENES: The Essenes were the ones that observed the signs of the times. They looked for political movements that may change or disrupt the status quo, and by these changes, they would see the Messiah coming to set up his kingdom.

The Pharisees asked Jesus certain questions to see where He stood so they could trap Him. The kingdom Jesus propagated was not futuristic, but Himself. The kingdom will not come about through passing more righteous laws, or righteous violence; it's not over there or or outside of us. Jesus said plainly "the kingdom of God is within"; it's God within you.[291] The poor, humble, and needy people of the lower classes saw the kingdom of God in Jesus, but the higher classes and Pharisees were scandalized by His righteous behavior. The application is foundational to us in our culture and society. Greg Boyd says, "The assumption that the kingdom could be more identified with a nation, verses another nation or all or any earthly nations, since it was Satan that rules over all nations and kingdoms,[292] is a profound mistake. Or that the kingdom is identified with passing more moral laws or righteous laws is also a profound mistake. It permeates the

---
291. Luke 17:21; Colossians 1:27.
292. Ephesians 2:2, 1 John 5:19, Revelation 17:18; 18:3.

church as where the church desires to pass righteous laws in order to control sinful behavior. Even our military expeditions become blessed by the church through patriotic emphasis. With mottos like, 'we are going to take America back to God,' which presupposes that we were always for God, or a holy and righteous nation to begin with. As if the United States as a nation was always fair and righteous for God. But the history shows otherwise as it existed during Puritanical times, or displacing American natives, or slavery. These didn't identify America as a Christian nation to begin with, though the Constitution was definitely what America should be."[293]

The kingdom cannot be identified by any of these ideologies or nations of the world. Jesus' kingdom is not of this world. Jesus said, "my kingdom is not of this world: if my kingdom were of this world, then would my servants fight, that I should not be delivered to the Jews: but now is my kingdom not from here."[294] The key point in this verse is that if Jesus' kingdom were anywhere in this world, then His angels would surely defeat anyone in His way. Instead, Jesus is describing a radical kingdom. It is a kingdom that loves enemies, and does not fight against them.

> *Realizing that we are in a spiritual battle, our focus should be based on taking up our cross, denying self, putting on Christ, and seeking His righteousness.*

The only fighting to be done is in a spiritual sense, as in Ephesians 6, by putting the full armor of God on, and even that, except perhaps for the sword, is for defense rather than offense. Recognizing that we are in a spiritual war is one thing, but the true fight, as Paul highlights in 2 Corinthians 10:4-5, is overcoming any false thinking that contradicts the authentic picture of God and bringing every thought under the authority of Christ. Solomon learned from this in that "as a man thinks, so is he."[295] Again, we need to recognize that only Christ in us can truly "fight against principalities and powers in dark places."[296] Only Jesus in us can exchange hate for love, common for holy, unrighteousness for rightness, resentment for forgiveness, and coveting for giving. Jesus is saying that this warfare is on a completely different level compared to how the nations of the world fight. That is why people are not the enemy, but rather the unseen forces of the "principalities and powers" are the enemy. Jesus said

---

293. See Greg Boyd's book, "Myth of a Christian Nation."
294. John 18:36.
295. Proverbs 23:7.
296. Ephesians 6:12.

to "Seek first the kingdom of God"[297] and allow God to deal with the other things of life: food, clothing, etc. Realizing that we are in a spiritual battle, our focus should be based on taking up our cross, denying self, putting on Christ, and seeking His righteousness. These are accomplished through allowing God to work in and through us in the Spirit. The question is: are we living the kingdom to all whom we meet, or are we just focused on our lives as dead people walking. The goal is to manifest the kingdom by breaking out of the dead lives we live and live in the newness of life that is more abundant, thereby approaching the center of the dome.

Thought Questions on Kingdom Centeredness

1) In what ways does denying ourselves for others affect our lives?

2) How can I constantly live under the dome of the King?

3) How can my circumstances change the way I view God?

4) How did Jesus handle the social issues of His time?

5) How do we compare God's kingdom to earthly kingdoms?

6) How is earthly warfare different from spiritual warfare?

7) Can earthly laws control sinful behavior? Why or why not?

---

297. Matthew 6:33.

The Counter Kingdom

God's kingdom is usually contrary to our presuppositions of what we believe it is or should be. Luke's gospel states that the kingdom is always looking for those who don't fit into society. "When one of those at the table with him heard this, he said to Jesus, Blessed is the one who will eat at the feast in the kingdom of God. Jesus replied: A certain man was preparing a great banquet and invited many guests. At the time of the banquet he sent his servant to tell those who had been invited, Come, for everything is now ready. But they all alike began to make excuses. The first said, I have just bought a field, and I must go and see it. Please excuse me. Another said, I have just bought five yoke of oxen, and I'm on my way to try them out. Please excuse me. Still another said, I just got married, so I can't come. The servant came back and reported this to his master. Then the owner of the house became angry and ordered his servant, Go out quickly into the streets and alleys of the town and bring in the poor, the crippled, the blind and the lame. Sir, the servant said, what you ordered has been done, but there is still room. Then the master told his servant, Go out to the roads and country lanes and compel them to come in, so that my house will be full. I tell you, not one of those who were invited will get a taste of my banquet."[298] The key point of this passage is to invite people who cannot repay. We have our social groups, and there is nothing

---

298. Luke 14:15-24, NET.

intrinsically wrong with that, but at the same time we must never forget about the people who may not fit into our social groups. They may not look like us, or they may have been marginalized or ostracized by society, and many times we pass over these marginalized people because they don't fit into our social circles. We need them in a paradoxical way for our continued Christian growth so that we can encourage others on their spiritual path. When we exclude these groups or others that are outside our social circles, we become myopic. A narrowed vision of being around only our social group prevents us from having an expanded mind for others. We need God's eyesight to break through our personal, habitual, and cultural boundaries. Jesus revealed that the lesson the Pharisees wanted to teach Him was reversed and He taught the Pharisees. For example, in the parable above, a Pharisee says, "Blessed is he that shall eat bread in the kingdom." However, Jesus turns it upside-down and invites diversity into His kingdom so that the kingdom is full. Verse 24 states that "none of those men that were bidden shall taste of my supper." Jesus is saying that religiosity and wealth have nothing to do with who sits at the table. In first-century Judaism, you identified whoever ate with you as your social group. In this parable, Jesus threw a banquet, and the Jewish people felt that it was only for them. Surprisingly, all the Jewish friends that Jesus invited to the banquet had excuses and the common thread running through them was that they were all too busy to come. After being insulted by all his Jewish "friends" Jesus decides to go everywhere to invite those who are societal outcasts. They would, through dining together, become part of his social group. This invitation is not based upon anything that the invitees have done, but rather on how gracious and merciful the host is with his abundant resources and the fact that he wants his house full. He doesn't care about your social standing, income, gender or race. The host wants to feed everyone, and anyone who responds to the invitation is accepted. It's as simple as that. The host told His servant to compel them to come in, and God desires His house to be full because of His love that compels them, not coerces them. God's love is never coercive or divisive.

The invitation to come as you are into the kingdom was for those people who were rejected by the Pharisees because of their condition. The Jews could not picture themselves with dirty, smelly misfits at their kingdom banquet table. The host had to ask the servant to compel them because these lower social groups would have a hard time believing that they were invited to the king's banquets. The fact that the king identifies with these groups tells us that it may be too difficult for the people to believe that it is true. Therefore, he sent a servant. In the antitypical account, the Host came down and identified with us in the person of His Son Jesus. He was the poorest of the poor; He had no possessions, nowhere to sleep, and most of His family abandoned Him. Therefore, He was able to connect with His invitees. Paul explains that it is God's love that draws and compels us.[299]

The original purpose of Israel was to extend this invitation to others and not make the banquet an exclusive right. Israel was chosen to be a nation of priests in order to show forth the beautiful character and grace of God, thereby attracting the world. However, since they failed, God has extended the call to His banquet to all who will respond to be priests and kings after His original priesthood. The barrier is broken, as Ephesians 2:14 states, and now all can partake of the priesthood extended to all believers.[300] Isaiah points out that the invitation was always there,[301] but Israel chose the exclusiveness as a badge of their righteousness. It came to the point that they began to judge the very people that they were told to serve. Even with this situation, God was patient, and throughout the Old Testament, He was trying, through His prophets, to get Israel to understand the difference of exclusiveness and inclusiveness.

God used prophet after prophet to bring them back to the single focus of their message, but Israel killed the messengers, so the Father decided to send his Son, but they killed the Master of the House, the Host of the banquet.[302] However, Jesus, through this parable, is identified with us so that we might receive His life. Christ brought forth the original invitation that was never fulfilled by the nation Israel, but now Christ fulfills it in and through Himself. Inviting all mankind is apparent in the new life in Christ, that all can participate by entering Christ, and when we enter into Christ, we enter into the new kingdom, and the fulfillment for us is to tell all others to enter into it as well. Jesus is the God that so truly represents His kingdom in comparison to all the other kingdoms on this earth. God's kingdom has no nationalistic tendencies or ethnic supremacy over another. He doesn't represent violence through earthly war to advance His kingdom, but rather He is a God that loves enemies. He transcends all preconceived ideas about His kingdom and breaks all social and ethical boundaries that mankind has set up. Christ embodies the character

---

299. 2 Corinthians 5:14, 15.
300. 1 Peter 2:9.
301. Isaiah 55:1-11.
302. Matthew 21:37-39.

of God, but those who behold or embrace only nationalism, violence, or and their social group will not will not see Him and His kingdom. They have rather created a false picture of God in their minds and reject the invitation. Those Pharisees who were with Jesus missed the mark on the invitation, but the lowly of society saw Jesus for who He was. Their hearts were open to Him, and their preconceived ideas didn't block the real Jesus when He invited them. The outsiders revealed that Jesus was on their side, especially when He died a criminal's death on the cross. He was an outcast of Rome, Israel, and the world. Mark said He was, *"numbered with the transgressors."*[303]

Until we feel the need to act upon the Word, profession means nothing. The Pharisees were always offended because Jesus broke religious, man-made rules, which was distasteful to their self-righteousness. The Pharisees became entrapped within the idol of their religion, nationalism, and self-assurance. How does this apply to us? A parable is centered on the fact that we identify with someone in the parable. The two groups we can see clearly are the ones that were expected to be there—Israel—and the ones that were not expected to be there—the outcasts, poor, prostitutes, disabled, and tax collectors. There is a warning to the first group and a promise to the second group. It pertains to the "insiders," though this isn't to take away from the already beautiful promises given to the church. The question is based on why we are assured and upon what do we stand. Do we look upon others as outsiders because we believe in Jesus, go to church, read the Bible and do this or that? Do we sometimes disdain outsiders, being prejudiced toward other people? Has our church become like an exclusive country club? Do we view ourselves as blessed, saved, and possessors of the truth, and not necessarily believe that the church is to be the servant to the world? On one level, we look inwardly to our health, wealth, and lives as a special people. On another level, we live in church cliques, have unconscious fears and feel we must protect our status in the church. Would we love our enemies? Would we pray for those who might hurt us? Remember the church is a people *called out* from the world, not a building.

Remember that was Israel's true role, to be servants to the world. It was all about revealing the character of God to the world. Our focus should be that as well. Despite what others think of us, whether in or out of the church, we should break social status and rank. Are our churches known for their humility and self-sacrificial love, not only to the world but toward each other in the church? Do we look like Jesus? Jesus attracted a small

---

303. Mark 15:28.

> *Remember that was Israel's true role, to be servants to the world. It was all about revealing the character of God to the world. Our focus should be that as well.*

number of people. Why? Because having a character like Jesus doesn't win popularity contests, but then again Jesus was never trying to win people through popularity anyway. He added value to their lives through a life-changing experience, and many could relate to Him because He was real, approachable, and authentic. They had the desire to be lifted out from their sin and Jesus was the one they could trust for the help they needed. As Jesus's love attracted the people, the Pharisees judged them. Jesus' holiness attracted sinners, in comparison to the Pharisees' self-righteousness and false holiness, which condemned and repelled sinners. It appears that sometimes the outcasts of society stay away from churches and Christianity as they did from the Pharisees of the first century. Judgment, condemnation, and a lack of love and humble servanthood in the church may apparently be seen by the outcasts. Therefore, to a major degree, outsiders may see more Pharisees than Jesus in the church. Humility and self-sacrificial love may lack to a significant degree within us because we are perhaps double-minded people and our focus isn't always on Christ.

Focusing on Jesus as we come under the King's dome is the only way to become like Him. Let us not recreate God in our minds, but rather be recreated in His mind.[304] When this happens, you will be changed into the same image from glory to glory, or from one level of godly character to another.[305] God desires us to manifest His love through our time, money, and resources, and His will is that we believe in Him to be able to do so.[306] The Beatitudes describe the mind needed by those who would receive the blessing: poor, humble, meek, pure in heart, poor in spirit, and peacemakers. The gospel sets itself against arrogance, haughtiness, pride, ego, and self-righteousness. We should all repeat Paul's words in 1 Timothy 1:15-16, recognizing that we are "chief of sinners," and what Jesus said in Matthew 7, that our sins are as logs in our eyes compared to the toothpicks of others. The kingdom, through the Spirit, tells us to see our sins as much greater than others. Therefore, it will become an honor to serve others, and if just a fraction of us did this through faith, the Father would

---

304. Philippians 2:5.
305. Romans 1:17.
306. See John 6:29.

be revealed to the world.

Therefore, we should not assume that we are the insiders unless we can answer the question, *"Why am I assured?"* God compels, implores, and motivates us to come to the table, and it's not based on anything that we did. Only those who truly respond realize the calling as the outcasts did in first-century Palestine. Desire to walk the kingdom call to the supper table, but remember, we may come as we are, but we will never leave as we are. All our confidence and assurance is rooted in the host of the banquet invitation.

Thought Questions on the Counter Kingdom

1) How can we ascribe worth to others when they don't fit into our social groups?

2) How do we grow by ascribing worth to all people?

3) Based on this chapter, how do we sometimes become like Pharisees?

4) What was the original purpose for Israel?

5) How do we have the tendency to recreate God in our own minds, rather than be created in His mind?

6) Based on this chapter, how do we sometimes view ourselves as "insiders"?

The Difference Between the Two Kingdoms

Jesus said in John 18:36, "My kingdom is not of this world: if my kingdom were of this world, then would my servants fight, that I should not be delivered to the Jews: but now is my kingdom not from hence." When Jesus was born, He entered the world among a political hotbed of issues such as Roman oppression, human right issues, and Jewish theological factions. Jesus knew that His kingdom would be viewed as radical by His Jewish people. Because their worldview of the kingdom did not match His, He expected confrontation and push back regarding His kingdom. The only ones that seemed to respond to His message were those from the lower social classes and who experienced the miracles He performed, including a Roman centurion.[307] Jesus came to build a countercultural kingdom. It's not that He desired to do this; it became that way only because of who He is and how people responded to His message. Also, the Israelites had lost sight of the true God for so long that they

> *Jesus came to build a countercultural kingdom. It's not that He desired to do this; it became that way only because of who He is and how people responded to His message.*

---

307. See Luke 7.

built their system of religion based on power and control.

Jesus' kingdom works on a totally different methodology than any kingdom on the earth. Jesus allowed Himself to be crucified to bring about the kingdom of God on earth. How strange it appears that the leader of a religion would begin his kingdom this way. Paul said that to those who are saved the "preaching of the cross is the power of God and yet foolishness to those who perish."[308] That which humans define as power, God turns upside-down. Jesus displayed at the cross the true power of God, an unconditional and unsurpassable love that ascribes worth to all. That's why Paul further said, "But we preach Christ crucified, unto the Jews a stumbling block, and unto the Greeks foolishness; But unto them which are called, both Jews and Greeks, Christ the power of God, and the wisdom of God. Because the foolishness of God is wiser than men; and the weakness of God is stronger than men."[309] The Greek word for stumbling block is *scandalon*. Jesus became a scandal to many and a byword of criticism and disdain. However, His call to all is to take up the cross and allow themselves to deny their basic, selfish, human, and natural tendencies. The scandal to the human flesh can't be more scandalous than to deny yourself, but even more scandalous, in the English equivalent, is becoming a stumbling block. Jesus was teaching that His kingdom is an under-kingdom, rather than an over-kingdom. After all, what can be more scandalous and more of a stumbling block than the expectation of your King to be crucified on a cross to start His kingdom? Jesus was to reveal the Father, and the cross was God's channel to do so.[310] Jesus taught that His kingdom is based upon love. He would show that love comes "under" people and not "over" them.[311] Those who are His disciples and preach the gospel by coming 'under' people through restoring them, cleansing them, and healing them, are bringing the life of Christ, the Kingdom of God, to them.[312] In Christ, when we come 'under' people, we use no coercion, manipulating techniques, force, or scare tactics, because none of these represent the kingdom of agape love. Jesus's kingdom is based on self-sacrificial love; therefore, it was fitting that Jesus said to Pilate, "my kingdom is not of this world."[313]

Napoleon Bonaparte, one of the leading conquerors and generals of this world, saw this aspect of Jesus and said this about Him and his

---

308. 1 Corinthians 1:18.
309. 1 Corinthians 1:23-25.
310. 1 Corinthians 1:18, 23, 24.
311. Galatians 5:22; 1 Timothy 1:15, Phil. 2:3,4.
312. Matthew 10:7, 8.
313. John 18:36.

kingdom: "I know men and I tell you that Jesus Christ is no mere man. Between him and every other person in the world there is no possible term of comparison. Alexander, Caesar, Charlemagne and I have founded empires. But on what did we rest the creations of our genius? Upon force. Jesus Christ founded his empire upon love; and at this hour millions of people would die for him."[314] Jesus revealed that His kingdom, built on His love, will have a polarizing effect on the world. Ellen White also said, "He (God) planned a government which would use no force; his subjects would know no oppression." She further said, "In the establishment of his government no carnal weapons were to be used, no coercion practiced; no attempt would be made to force the consciences of men."[315] Only love compels true obedience.

Therefore, the goal of Jesus, found in 1 Corinthians 12, is to have a body where He is the head and of His body, which lives under His kingdom where all the principles of His government are based on love. The fruit of the Spirit display the attributes that flow from His love and become one with us. In Him, both individually and collectively, we become a body of believers, unified in love, allowing His self-denying divine nature within us. The degree with which we love our enemies is the degree to which we have His divine nature in us. This was the prerequisite to what Paul said: "examine yourself to see if you are in the faith."[316]

To the degree that we love our enemies is the degree to which we have His divine nature in us.

Jesus said in Matthew 5 that we are to "love our enemies and pray for them so that you will become children like your Father in heaven."[317] Jesus desires that this example of His love be reproduced in all His followers so that they become true children of God, and to the extent that it is reproduced in us is the extent to which we become God's children. Martin Luther King Jr. once compared forgiveness with the capacity to love. He said, "We must develop and maintain the capacity to forgive. He who is devoid of the power to forgive is devoid of the power to love."[318]

---

314. Napoleon Bonaparte, *Napoleon's argument for the divinity of Christ and the Scriptures: in a conversation with General Bertrand, at St. Helena* (Charleston, SC: South Carolina Tract Society, 1861).
315. Ellen White, *"The Kingdom of Christ,"* The Advent Sabbath and Review and Herald. Vol. 73, no. 33. Aug. 18, 1896
316. 2 Corinthians 13:5.
317. Matthew 5:44, 45.
318. Martin Luther King Jr. spoke this in a sermon called "Loving Your Enemies". It was spoken on Christmas Day in 1957 in the Dexter Avenue Baptist Church in Montgomery, Alabama.

We can see Jesus' intent on reproducing this power of love and forgiveness in His disciples. Simon was a zealot and zealots hated tax collectors like Matthew. They hated the Roman government and desired all to take up arms to destroy and kill for the kingdom of God.

However, in comparison, tax collectors benefited from the Roman power. They thought the Romans were okay people and they didn't want the political boat to be rocked. Jewish tax collectors worked directly for the Roman government to collect taxes from their people. The Romans figured it would be better to have nationals to collect taxes rather than themselves, and it became a shrewd political move on the part of the Romans. Often tax collectors would charge more to make a profit, and the Romans couldn't care less, as long as they received their required quota. That is why Jewish people hated tax collectors. Matthew was different from Simon the zealot, and they came from different political views and standings. It would be like putting a liberal with an ultra-conservative today; but Jesus still said "follow me" to both of them, and He was confident that the under-kingdom, based on His love, would be more powerful than an over-kingdom movement that all of the nations in the world have adopted. As in this case, Jesus' words come true again as He speaks in the Gospel of John: "A new commandment I give unto you, that ye love one another; as I have loved you, that you also love one another. By this shall all men know that ye are my disciples, if ye have love one to another."[319] Therefore, the kingdom of love is an under-kingdom movement that changes people's hearts so that they desire to become a disciple of Jesus. It is a fruit that comes straight from agape love. Jesus was teaching all His disciples a different kind of kingdom. When Jesus becomes Lord of our lives, and we live under His dome, then the differences that stem from worldly kingdoms, like in Simon and Matthew's case, become marginal and the similarities instigated by the heavenly kingdom become awakened and alive.

These two worldly kingdoms, one from the world and the other from God, are like oil and water, and only through the Spirit of God directing and guiding us into holy things do we then become one kingdom under Christ. Simon and Matthew were represented like oil and water, and only through the Spirit of God directing and guiding both into holy things could they become one new kingdom under Christ. Though Simon and Matthew were separated by two worldly ideologies, they were unified under Christ's Kingdom, a Kingdom of unifying love. Again, the kingdoms of the world use the power *over* people, such as the sword, coercion, and threats. The

---

319. John 13:34, 35.

power of the kingdom of God is *under-oriented*; it is a power of humility and radical love.

Several years ago, I read about a man who murdered several children at a small, Amish, one-room schoolhouse in Lancaster County, Pennsylvania. Several facets of God's agape love came out in that story related to loving our enemies. The gunman let out a teacher and some other girls and boys and then barricaded himself in the schoolhouse with the intent to kill the rest of the girls. A thirteen-year-old girl named Marian Fisher stood up and requested to be shot first, in the hopes that her sisters and others who were with her would be spared. She was overheard by the survivors as saying, "Shoot me and let the other ones loose." The gunman shot and killed Marian. As soon as her lifeless body hit the floor her younger, eleven-year-old sister, Barbie, stood up and said, "Shoot me next," hoping to save the other girls as well. She was wounded in the hand, leg, and shoulder, but survived. Charles Roberts killed the five remaining girls and critically wounded the other five before turning the gun on himself and ending his life.

However, it is the courage and faith of Marian and Barbie that will be remembered. Love is forsaking self; it is not afraid and doesn't seek to protect itself. It is an outrageous love that gives to others.[320] As amazing as Marian and Barbara's faith was, just as amazing was the faith of the Amish community. They demonstrated agape love in action, without any reservations or second thoughts. They gathered to raise money for the killer's family, and rumors were that even the father of one of the victims was a pallbearer for the gunman since he had no friends and a small family. The World Net Daily reported, "In what's being called a stunning example of 'the imitation of Christ,' the Amish community, devastated by the cold-blooded murder of five of its schoolgirls, is raising money for the killer's family. Amish residents of rural Lancaster County, Pa., have started a charity fund to help not only the victims' families – but also the mass murderer's widow and children... Dwight Lefever, a spokesman for the Roberts family, said an Amish neighbor comforted the killer's family and extended forgiveness to them after the shooting."[321] And columnist Rod Dreher, reacting to the Amish outpouring of support for the killer's family, wrote: "Yesterday on NBC News, I saw an Amish midwife who had helped birth several of the girls murdered by the killer say that they

---

320. John 15:13.
321. WorldNet Daily, "Grieving Amish raise money for Killer's Family: This is possible if you have Christ in your heart." October 4, 2006.

were planning to take food over to his family's house. She said—and I paraphrase closely—'This is possible if you have Christ in your heart.'"[322]

This demonstration of the Amish is but a small example in a sinful world of how Christ's death and resurrection give power to come "under" people. Though there may be collateral damage, God demonstrated that agape love is a picture of who He is, and through the death of the Amish children, a picture of God went forth to the community and the world. Love is a powerful tool as a witness for Christ. We are given the ability, in Christ, to love as God loves, and as the Amish people in this story understood, the way to stay free from evil and combat it was to bless the victims of this situation. Such is another example of true freedom in Christ.

The end will only come when the gospel is preached as a witness.[323] In other words, when the world sees the gospel lived out in people's lives, then the end will come. Love lived out has a polarizing effect. When we become vulnerable and authentic in Christ, it's usually at those times we grow spiritually. It's a freeing and restorative power that comes *'under'* and not *'over'* people. It's the power to imitate who Jesus is and not who Caesar is. The power over mode is of Satan's kingdom and Satan himself. Jesus acknowledged and never disputed that Satan owned all the kingdoms.[324] The kingdoms of the world are based on the flesh, and the intentions of worldly kingdoms are based on my rights ("What's in it for me?"). In contrast, the kingdom of God is built through the Spirit in Jesus, which leads us to die daily. The kingdom of God is motivated by love for others and not love for self or my selfish interests. Paul charged us to "think of others as being better than yourselves."[325] The kingdom of God ascribes worth to others, whereas the kingdoms of this earth are defined by threats of law or power over others. Since only Christ in us can esteem others better than ourselves, we must conclude we have no innate power to love enemies or count others worth more than we are. Only Christ in us has the capability and capacity to love enemies. On a human level, our nature coerces, manipulates, and forces behavior to conform, whereas in God's kingdom unconditional love through the Spirit influences people to change.

> **When we become vulnerable and authentic in Christ, it's usually at those times we grow spiritually.**

---

322. Associated Press, "Amish girl asked to be shot first to save Classmates," Saturday, October 7, 2006.
323. Matthew 24:14.
324. See 1 John 5:19; Revelation 17:18; 18:3.
325. Philippians 2:3, ISV.

The power 'over' kingdom doesn't care about our motives or behavior, whether they be fear or belief in conformity. The concept of coercion and manipulation just cares about a behavioral change and not a heart change. Neither does it care about our inner state of being, ethics, or choices. Conform, or you will receive pain, starvation, or death—it's as simple as that. It's almost always a fear-based motive of obedience. The kingdom *'under'* being under God's dome of His kingdom, is not interested so much in external behavior, but rather an internal restoration and transformation. God desires to change our hearts through dwelling within us in self-sacrificial love. Worldly kingdoms are built upon nationalistic and ethnic groups. The fallen flesh sets these parameters, usually based on coveting the highest positions. The competition of the spirit of the flesh is always one of hierarchy, supremacy, and competition. It's an intrinsic aspect of our flesh and all the kingdoms of the world. However, in God's kingdom, since Jesus died for all,[326] every being has absolute worth and infinite value. Therefore, our goal is to show forth and express through the Spirit to others the worth of the cross. The worldly kingdoms create enemies, but the heavenly kingdom forbids us to have enemies. The kingdoms of the world are about conflict, whereas the kingdom of heaven is about personal reconciliation.[327] If God doesn't point out people's personal sins, then neither should we. This allows for reconciliation and restoration to take place.

The true kingdom replicates Calvary through reconciliation to one another and the world. We should continually consider the question, *Do we exemplify a Calvary-quality love to reconcile others to Christ?* Love is the defining mark of peace, joy, and unity. We may have differences, but these attributes mark the real Christian through love, joy, and peace, and Jesus is the Truth. Therefore, our opinions of the world should never be synonymous with the heavenly kingdom. Why is that true? Because only in the truth as 'it is written,' is there true light, power, love, joy, and peace. When the kingdoms of the world and the appearance of God's kingdom are fused, both civil and religious, then the kingdoms of this world are in 'over' or coercive mode, apparently suppressing God's kingdom. That's why we separate ourselves from the world kingdoms and contrast it by God's kingdom of love. The beauty is that God's kingdom wins because of that. It appears that it makes no sense to think that, but Paul said, "And having disarmed principalities and powers he mocked them openly, and triumphed over

---

326. 2 Corinthians 5:14, 15; Rom. 6:19; 1 Tim. 2:6; Heb. 7:27,10:10.
327. 2 Corinthians 5:19-21; Ephesians 2:13-16.

them."[328] In other words, Satan thought that through coercion, force, and manipulation that he would win the great controversy, but by Christ coming 'under' and not 'over,' God put Satan's method to open shame. Paul said in 1 Corinthians that this mystery was hidden from the ages which God destined before the world began which none of the rulers of this world understood, otherwise they would have never crucified Christ. Ironically, Satan's plan backfired on him, and love won. Praise God!

John states that only through true, unconditional agape love will the world know who the real Christians are.[329] God has put into the church a witness for Him in the form of a unified body, and this body becomes an army for the Lord.[330] Jesus said in John.17:23, "I in them, and thou in me, that they may be made perfect in one; and that the world may know that thou hast sent me, and hast loved them, as thou hast loved me." The reason for this unity is for the world "to know." Jesus prayed that the incarnate Godhead would incarnate Himself in us and that a mutual indwelling (*perichoresis*) would take place. The same unity in love that the Godhead shares is available for us, for the revelation of the character of God.

When the church receives the out-pouring of the latter rain, one attribute will be clear, and that is the world will see in the unified church a self-sacrificial, Calvary love. As previously mentioned, to the extent that this happens, the world will be polarized, and it will attract some and others will feel condemned by it, but the fact remains that Jesus will be seen in His people. The world will see that they are recipients of a radical love which unifies His people. Therefore, the big question is: are we willing to allow this daily, mutual indwelling to take place in our lives?

Even though the two kingdoms are distinct and must be distinct, we still must remember that we are all missionaries, and a missionary is a person on a mission. Being a missionary in America can at times be difficult because 70% or more of the people who declare themselves as Christian don't live up to the faith they profess.[331] It's not easy to be a missionary in America because it's hard to determine who is 'in' and who is 'out.' Some people who we think are "in" may be "out" and some that are "out" may be closer to "in" than we think. Profession means nothing to God. That's why living our beliefs and convictions means everything. The United States may have the most Christians as a nation and the most

---

328. Colossians 2:15, EMTV.
329. John 13:35.
330. Joel 2.
331. 2014 Pew Research study.

people going to church, but we are one of the most immoral countries on the planet. The kingdom of God happens when change comes from within. Don't think you can take the murder out of a murderer's heart by passing a law. Only God can turn a sinner into a saint. Could a law be passed against those who steal and would it do any good? No, we already have those laws. Yes, some may fear jail time and paying legal fees as deterrents, but it still may be in their hearts. How successfully are their hearts reformed against stealing while allowing prison to "rehab" them? Not very good. Only God can take away the desire to steal, kill, lie, etc. God changes hearts and minds from the inside through agape love. Even the prodigal son's heart was changed when he realized how beautiful his father's love was when he was feeding the pigs. And it was at that very moment that he realized that his father was ever so loving to his servants that he decided he would return.

> *The kingdom of God happens when change comes from within. Don't think you can take the murder out of a murderer's heart by passing a law. Only God can turn a sinner into a saint.*

We have a directive from God to divide the holy from the common as 2 Timothy 2:3-4 states: "You therefore must endure hardness, as a good soldier of Jesus Christ, no soldier on duty entangles himself in matters of everyday life; otherwise he will not please the one who recruited him." During first-century Roman times, soldiers were usually posted in foreign countries where they were enticed to leave their post or even their positions totally and be freed from the rule of Rome. That is where this verse comes into play in our lives. We are in a spiritual war in a foreign world where our commanding officer, Jesus, desires us not to become so entangled in this world because Satan is always pulling at us to leave our post. However, God desires us to focus like good soldiers on our duties as we battle. God calls us to glorify and please Him, and as good soldiers, we should always please our enlisting officer.

Thought Questions on the Difference Between the Two Kingdoms

1) How was Jesus' teaching countercultural?

2) How can our view of Jesus become a stumbling block?

3) How do the two kingdoms differ?

4) In what ways are you affected by God's kingdom?

5) Describe Jesus' 'under' movement versus Satan's 'over' movement.

6) Describe a characteristic of the 'under' movement that would apply to you.

7) What are the dangers of fusing the two kingdoms?

The King's Kingdom

The King's kingdom is all about walking in the awareness of God. Usually, we might pray for fifteen minutes or so in the morning, then before you know it we're on our way to work, and then we're mad at the person in the car in front us who cut us off. Wouldn't it be nice to have His peace and power throughout the day, not just briefly in the morning? Many of us fall into a robotic mind and default to our human nature. We forget the physical world around us and are focused on our needs for the day. We become what I call, "temporary" or "conditionalist" atheists. We live throughout our day oblivious or half asleep to the Spirit. Being conscious and awake of the Kingdom all the time is taking every thought captive to Christ.[333] When Jesus calls us to love the unlovable, we may in our minds judge them; when He calls us to pray for those that spitefully use and abuse us, we may retaliate in our minds and perhaps execute an outward display of it as well. We're usually easily distracted, rather than walking in a kingdom awareness. The King of the dome desires us to partake in His domain and the only way that can be done, as we stated earlier, is to live every second of our lives with the living Christ in us. Putting on His mind, praying without ceasing, and walking in the Spirit are what Paul describes as crucial for our experiential walk of faith. The question we need to ask ourselves is, *Do we daily live in an outrageous servant mentality through love?* For the

---

333. 2 Corinthians 10:5.

most part, our walk is as if that isn't true. Our minds are fragmented. We might be aware of God's love in the worship service, prayer meeting, and Bible study, but perhaps struggle throughout our daily lives.

Too many times we compartmentalize our faith. God calls us to integrate our faith with our everyday lives, but we seem to be walking through life half-asleep. Walking in God's love toward others is revolutionary; it changes our perspective and reinforces the kingdom view. We are no longer defined by the circumstances around us, but rather by God's love in us, which in turn gives spiritual impact to those around us. It brings joy, peace, and a profound love that didn't previously exist. Walking in the light is a moment-by-moment experience of renewing our mind constantly, and when that happens, we walk in the Spirit. All these relate to continual and mutual indwelling. Unfortunately, as stated, it appears that sometimes we walk in the spirit and then walk out of the spirit. We all desire this consistent walk with Christ, even bringing every thought into captivity to the obedience of Christ. As we previously saw, Paul was driven by the unique love of God, considering that it's "the love of Christ that compels us."[334]

The Greek word *sunecho* means 'compel' or "to surround something" to make it move forward. It motivated Paul to do what he did. It should be the only motivation for what every Christian does. However, when we do "life," the tendency is to get sucked into the world of distractions, and our motivation gets lost.

The reason why God's love compelled Paul is that he was convicted that Jesus died for all, including him. Paul didn't see people in terms of what Adam did, but rather what Christ did. That's why Paul said, "from now on we do not think of anyone from a human point of view."[335] In other words, Paul was convicted that we need to treat all people as Jesus would treat us. We are not contending against 'flesh' or a human opponent but rather against 'spiritual forces, principalities, and powers.' The conviction of Christ's love compelled Paul to live in a unique and different way because Paul saw that God gave all humanity worth. When we catch the vision that God has for us, in that God valued each person with an unsurpassable and unconditional worth, then we will become convicted that God's love has compelled us to see all people with that same unsurpassable and unconditional worth as well. When we become convicted of this on a moment-by-moment basis, then we no longer live in the common but rather in the holy, and we won't live in recognition of ourselves, but

---

334. 2 Corinthians 5:14, EMTV.
335. 2 Corinthians 5:16, ISV.

rather we will live under the dome of the King, thereby pulling us from self and giving us the desire to live more attentively for others. This is the abundant life that Jesus spoke of in John 10:10. It is the 'real' life, and this life sets us free from ourselves. As the Spirit works in our lives, we become more aware of others' needs and less of our needs and wants.

Paul lived for others because he was convicted that Jesus died for all. The questions are: Are you convicted that Jesus died for all? And that He is the exact character[336] of God, dying on the cross? It doesn't just matter if you believe it because most people would answer yes to that question. Rather, are you convicted by it? Will it permeate your whole life? Every waking minute can be given over to God so that He allows this experience to happen. God desires to frame our lives into holiness rather than just common activity throughout the day. When you wake up in the morning, is your mind on God, or only on what needs to be accomplished that day? No matter your circumstance or situation, whether it be death, cancer, loved ones dying, or anger from loved ones or friends, do you still believe that God extends this loving picture of Himself toward you? Are you convicted by it? It is only through "faith established by love"[337] that you can become convicted by it. And the question to us is: Are we single-minded,[338] or does our mind flash pictures that are inconsistent with the life of Christ or the kingdom? How long do we hold onto those pictures? The key is to keep our brains from the trash of the world, culture, our genetics, our work, etc., which have a direct impact on our experience and picture of God. Too many times we allow the externals to shape and mold our God picture. Also, the problem is that our minds run on autopilot throughout the day, shaped by what it beholds, and point us in certain directions that are inconsistent with who we desire to be. Many times, we are unaware of it, because of the habits that are already formed in our minds. Because of these, unfortunately, many times our picture of God is then distorted, i.e., God is arbitrary, unfair, and unjust, and our faith becomes crippled.

The reality is that we cannot live and experience God's unsurpassable worth if we have an ugly picture of God. I can't live in love, as Christ loved me and gave Himself for me, if my picture of God is distorted because otherwise, I won't trust God, as compared to what happened to Adam and Eve. Rather, I can believe that God does have my best interest and loves me.

---

336. Hebrews 1:3.
337. Galatians 5:6.
338. Romans 8:6.

When Paul spoke the famous words in Romans 12:2, "don't be conformed to the world but rather be transformed by the renewing of your minds (hearts)," he was referring to the fact that God desires to transform our hearts in the light of His redeeming love. When this happens, it will reveal God's will for our lives. God's love is a redemptive love, so much so that it will permeate our whole behavior and put us on track, knowing God's will as He unfolds it to us. Paul says in 1 Corinthians 13 that "whatever we do, do in love." Therefore, as a truly healthy motivating force, the only thing is love. It's the underlying motive to stop fear, guilt, and shame. Paul said that 'love does no wrong to its neighbor' because 'love is the fulfillment of the law.'[339] The reason why God's love becomes the motive is that God's love has an everlasting impact. Paul lived by God's goodness because it changed him. God's covenant has always been based on love. "God's goodness or kindness leads us to repentance," and that 'goodness' changes us to free us from ourselves and our self-centered thoughts, at the same time giving hope to others. God's love will motivate and change us, despite our self-centered and self-destructive ways. We should never use guilt, fear, shame, and threats as a motivating factor to be convinced God loves us. Rather, we can experience God's love amid fear, shame, guilt, and bondage. God's love becomes the center of our experience as it pushes out fear. Love fills the Law full of meaning and Jesus filled the Law full of Love.

It's true that the obedience that springs forth from fear, guilt, and shame only produces the character of a rebel in the end. The other side of the coin is that we should never use God's love to keep us in sin. The modern movement of "I'm OK you're OK," diffuses God's convicting love that would otherwise free a person from the bondage of sin. Many people have fallen for a cynical, self-deceptive form of a false love. God's true love has the motivation to expel the bondage of sin from our lives. God's love is the essence of who He is. Love transcends all of His attributes. In other words, all of God's attributes flow from His character of love. Love fulfills the law, it is where faith receives it's power, it defines Jesus, Christians are motivated by it. God loves enemies and unites peoples. His love transcends knowledge, never fails, is patient, is kind, and I can go on and on.[340] Again, "it was for freedom that Christ set us free."[341] Everything in the Christian life depends on conviction through faith in the love of God.

---

339. Romans 13:10, NET.
340. Galatians 5:6; 1 John 3:16; 2 Corinthians 5:14; 1 John 4:8; Matthew 5:44; Ephesians 3:19; 1 Corinthians 13:4, 8.
341. Galatians 5:1.

John said that "God is love... and perfect love expels fear."[342] If God's love is not in the center of our hearts to expel fear, then fear will give into hopelessness and pain. Our picture of God in our minds must be freed from human presuppositions about God's love. Also, we must not form a picture of God from our negative, personal, past experiences. That's why the first thing Satan attacked was Eve's picture of God.

As previously mentioned, the serpent used words to change the picture of God in her mind. Satan basically said, "God lied, you won't surely die. God held back. He doesn't want you to become like him, but you will become gods, knowing good and evil." Therefore, Eve now saw that the food on the tree was "good" to "make one wise" and she "delighted" in it. The word in Hebrew for delight is *tahavaw* and it means "lust or covet." Satan changed Eve's view from one of total dependence on God to coveting and lusting. By changing Eve's picture of God, it wasn't hard for Satan to convince Eve to eat of the tree. Both Adam and Eve became like gods because they started the pattern and form of self-worship on this earth. Satan gave the impression that God is a liar, threatened by the tree, and doesn't have Adam and Eve's best interest at heart, when in reality, Satan painted the lie about God and continues with his lies up until this day, even until the day of destruction. He painted an ugly picture of God, and a deceptive one, one that portrays God as selfish. Ever since that day, the distortion of the true picture of God has continued. Regarding the choices of good and evil within us, Dietrich Bonhoeffer said, "Bearing within himself the knowledge of good and evil, man has become judge over God and men, just as he is judge over himself."[343]

The good news is that there will be a people that will characterize God and bring into the world a correct, accurate, true picture of God who is loving, merciful, compassionate, and longsuffering. By eating of the tree, Adam and Eve plunged this world into a self-idolatrous picture of the god they wanted to create because of Satan's lie. Soon the world will see what the true character of God is because there will be a people who will have been fully recreated in God's image through His mind, through His indwelling presence.

Therefore, to the extent of our conviction of God's love is the extent to which we are compelled. We know that God loves, but are we convicted of God's love, so it compels us? The devils believe and tremble, but they will never be convicted about God's love to compel them to do what is right.

---

342. 1 John 4:16-18.
343. Dietrich Bonhoeffer, *Ethics* (New York: Simon and Schuster, 1995), 29.

God will meet us where we are to remove any obstacle of fear, hate, anger, etc., so that we can better and more fully experience His love, thereby compelling us to greater levels of His compassion.

Thought Questions on the King's Kingdom

1) What does it mean to walk in kingdom awareness?

2) How does God compel us to walk in spiritual awareness?

3) How does one become convicted that Jesus died on the cross for them?

4) How can your view of God change your behavior?

5) What happens when God's love is not in the center of your heart?

6) What does it mean to be double-minded?

7) How can we bring our minds back when they wander into common life?

8) In what way did God's love compel Paul?

9) What expels fear from our lives and why?

10) How do we sometimes eat from the tree of good and evil?

11) How can we integrate our faith into our everyday lives? Provide three examples.

The Discerning Kingdom

The defining feature of God's Kingdom children is that they clothe themselves every day in the love that God displayed on the cross. Jesus ascribed to us an unsurpassable worth with His willingness to pay the ultimate price for us when we were in a condition undeserving of it. That is genuine agape love; that is the kind of God that displays the root of His eternal nature. When we invite God into us and allow him to implant His divine nature in us, then we take on the character of Christ. Entering His life at this point, we then begin to acquire the Calvary love of Christ. With the focal point being the self-sacrificial love of Christ, we can't help but be patterned after His life if we but behold Him. By fixing our eyes on Christ, we become a people who are willing to sacrifice our own time, resources, energy, and even lives for the sake of others, regardless of whether they are our friend or foe.

Whether others benefit us or threaten us, it doesn't matter, because God's self-sacrifice displays a unilateral love that flows outward, just as we saw with the Amish community. It's a unilateral and unconditional love through which we ascribe an unsurpassable worth toward others, at a cost to ourselves when necessary and appropriate. Jesus said in Matthew 5 that we should love our enemies and bless those who hate us in order that we can be children of our Father in heaven. The words "in order" are a bridge that conveys a transition. John says the same thing, "Behold what manner of love has the father bestowed upon us that we should be called the children of God."[344] The beholding becomes the most distinguishing mark of the kingdom. In other words, loving our enemies proves we have the Father's love in us. The key habit is to daily, and moment-by-moment, put on agape love, the life of Christ. Paul says that if we do not love like this, then there is nothing that is worth anything. You can have all the right beliefs, supernatural faith, and work miracles, but if it's not motivated by love, then it is altogether worthless.[345]

> *By fixing our eyes on Christ, we become a people who are willing to sacrifice our own time, resources, energy, and even lives for the sake of others, regardless of whether they are our friend or foe.*

This is the foundation of the kingdom—a love that loves enemies. God redefines love in our world. The present-day Amish and Mennonites pull their heritage from the Anabaptists. The Anabaptist people who lived in the early sixteenth century were persecuted by almost all denominations, Catholic and Protestant alike. The word *'Ana'* means *'again,'* so the name "Anabaptist" means to be baptized again. In the world in which they lived, infant baptism was still a major doctrine that Catholics and Protestants were not ready to give up, but the Anabaptists believed in adult baptism. Therefore, the most popular way to kill Anabaptists was to drown them. It was a cruel and evil way to die, stated by their persecutors: *'well if you believe that you need to be baptized again we will drown you.'* However, they were known for loving their enemies, and were the only sect in the middle ages that did not retaliate against their enemies.

The main obstacle to God's love in our life is that we eat of the tree of the knowledge of good and evil. That's why when we judge what is right or wrong, it blocks us from God's love. When we eat of the forbidden tree, we then become gods and begin to think as gods by judging others. And judgment of ourselves blocks the flow of God's love to us just as much as judging others. Judgment collapses the flow of love to others, whereas when we love others it collapses judgment. We are to be recreated to be like God in how we love, but instead, we become like Satan in how we judge. The minute we do that, we can no longer be like God. Only God can love *and* judge perfectly. For the rest of us, it's incompatible with our fallen human nature to

---

344. 1 John 3:1.
345. 1 Corinthians 13:1-3; See also Galatians 5:6.

> *Only God can love and judge perfectly. . . . Judgment is about ascribing worth toward ourselves at the cost of others, and love is ascribing worth to others at cost to ourselves.*

do so. Judgment is about ascribing worth toward ourselves at the cost of others, and love is ascribing worth to others at cost to ourselves. When we judge, we contrast ourselves with others. And we may think, *we're not like that, we are truly Christian people, right believing people, unlike those people.* But most of the time we ascribe worth to ourselves at the cost of others. It's the opposite of love, the antithesis of love. Again, true love is about ascribing worth to others at a cost to ourselves.

Judgment blocks the flow of God's love. If we are going to be a people who love as God does, we are going to have to be a people who stifle all judgment. Ninety-six percent of all our judgment takes place in our heads and it changes and affects our behavior, because our judgment blocks the flow of God's love to our minds, and we then end up ascribing worth toward ourselves rather than others. Unless we have close friends to whom we can give advice, without judging, then the only attitude that we need toward others is to treat them as God treats us and that is ascribing worth toward them. We ascribe worth toward others, manifesting God's love towards them, in how we treat them, speak about them, and think about them. The more we allow and partake of God's love, then the more judgment of others is subdued.

Judgment blocks the flow of displaying the beauty of Christ's character to others. The principles in 1 Corinthians 4:3-5 are so liberating, yet they are hardly ever discussed. Unfortunately, mainstream Christian religion embodies judgment, but the true gospel liberates us from judgment. Paul says, "It is a minor matter that I am judged by you or by any human court. In fact, I do not even judge myself. For my conscience is clear, but that does not vindicate me. It is the Lord who judges me. So then, do not judge anything before the time. Wait until the Lord comes. He will bring to light the hidden things of darkness and reveal the motives of the heart. Then each will receive praise from God." In verse 3 Paul says he doesn't even judge himself. Though he has a clear conscience, he knows that doesn't make him innocent. Paul doesn't even trust his mind when assessing his life. He feels innocent, though that doesn't mean he his. Paul comes to the point of realizing that it is the Lord who judges him. It's the Lord who judges everyone. Therefore, judge nothing before the appointed time. We need to wait until the Lord comes when He will bring to light what is hidden in darkness and expose the motives of the heart. At that time everyone will receive their praise from God. In other words, there will be a judgment and God alone will judge. Until that time comes, we don't have the right to judge or assess people. God alone can reveal the hidden things in our hearts and those of others. We, as humans, should have no part in playing God. Appearances can be very deceiving, yet on that day, everything will be known. That's why Jesus said to forgive them, for they don't know what the real war is all about. Only the love of God will purify what needs to be purified and destroy that which needs to be destroyed. This is a declaration of freedom from judging.

Again, Paul says that He doesn't judge anyone, including himself; therefore he says not to judge anyone before the Lord comes back. Furthermore, Ephesians 6 says we are not fighting against flesh, but rather principalities and powers in the heavenly realms. In other words, we can't declare any enemy in the flesh because the spiritual warfare we are in only relates to demonic forces against God. That's why Paul says in 2 Corinthians 5:16 that he doesn't think of anyone from a human standpoint. Paul understands, as should we, that we are not fighting against other humans, but spiritual forces that only desire to seek and destroy humans.

There is a bondage in living an addiction that assesses, evaluates, and thinks critically of others. Love stops the gossip within our minds and frees us from any speculation, for only God knows the truth. Most of the time we are so used to it that we don't even know were doing it. So many times, we contrast who we are with others, and our assessment usually puts us on the top. These tendencies need to be thwarted for us to bless others. We need to stop ourselves when we think, *Oh look at that so and so, I can't believe that person,* etc. Each of those thoughts blocks the flow of God in us and through us. It's bondage, and only when it's stifled in our lives can we have true freedom from it. The accuser, Satan, has made a lot of little accusers out of us.

Paul sees that when we genuinely trust God to be the judge of the earth, and our whole identity is in Jesus Christ, then we can set all earthly assessment and judgment of others aside. We just need to live in love right now. God will take care of the rest, and only to the degree that we set aside all our judgments, assessments, and evaluations of others can we then live in the love in which God desires us to live. Try it. It's very liberating and freeing. Remember, all judgment blocks the flow of God's love. Only by looking through the lens of the cross do we have the power of the cross, which is living in the reality and freedom of the cross. Let's face it—it's hard to take the burden and play God through judging. Assessing and judging is a burden that God never intended for us to have. Satan can even make us feel guilty of letting that go. He comes into our minds and prompts us to think that we are helping others by doing it. Our reasoning may be that we may feel guilty if we don't judge because then we may feel as if we are condoning sin, as though we are sinless. Remember it was for freedom that Christ set us free.[346] Even if people threaten our freedom in Christ, God will take care of that too. We don't need to take judgment or even justice into our hands. Romans 12 says to leave it all to God, set aside vengeance, make room for God's wrath, don't crowd God out with your wrath, and love your enemy. We can only do that if we are freed from all diabolical assessment. Ellen White stated, "the only condition upon which the freedom of man is possible is that of becoming one with Christ."[347] Therefore, put on Christ every moment.

> *Only by looking through the lens of the cross do we have the power of the cross, which is living in the reality and freedom of the cross.*

However, there is a good and necessary judgment. The Greek word *krino* means "judgment." The root of it means to separate and distinguish. From *krino* we get the English word "critic'". The bad judgment from the knowledge of the tree of good and evil is a separation of people, where we separate ourselves from others to feed our egos and make us feel better than they are. The good judgment is that we separate things and not people. We distinguish between what is true or false and what is consistent with the kingdom and what is contrary to the kingdom. Hebrews 5:14 states, "but solid food is for the mature Christian, whose minds are trained through practice to distinguish what is right and wrong or the good from the evil." The experienced Christian, Paul says, can assess what is of the kingdom and what is not. Judging behavior doesn't mean judging people, but rather exhorting them through love and lifting them up to be healed and restored in Christ. Furthermore, mature Christians see themselves as lower than others. As we see ourselves as the worst of sinners, whatever sins we see in others are more modest. This is the sign of a maturity that we have trained our minds to attain. This discernment is to characterize the body of Christ. We need to have in the body a people who can help others gain discernment, otherwise, we can't grow spiritually as desired.

---

346. Galatians 5:1.
347. The Desire of Ages, p. 466.

The early church was made up of house churches that consisted of about twenty to thirty people each. They knew each other intimately, and if something came up which was inconsistent with the Christian walk, then an assessment was made, edifying not only what was best for that individual, but also what was best for the body of believers. Peter says that "judgment must begin at the house of God.[348]" Many have only viewed this verse as it relates to where judgment begins when truth is present; however, I believe there must be a people who can discern for edification purposes in the house of God. This is not to say that the church becomes the moral police of the world, but rather spiritual discernment, for edification purposes, begins at the house of God. And Paul affirms this by saying: "for it is no business of mine to be judging those who are outside (of the church)"[349] Obviously, Paul is saying we have no business judging people outside of the church. Holding those "outside" accountable to the standards of the kingdom when they didn't confess to being Christians is not our job. Instead, we need to discern, in a loving way, what evil in the church destroys the body of believers and help them. The church is called to live as the faithful bride of Christ. Paul points this out to the Corinthian church when one man is sleeping with his mother-in-law. This, Paul says, is to be brought out because it's inconsistent with the kingdom, but those outside the church are not to be judged. The church is not to pass their laws upon the others of the land who do not ascribe to Christian beliefs. The early church was structured for good discernment because most were small churches meeting in homes. Furthermore, the church was the people and not a building, whereas 90% or more of Christians today believe it to be a building and it is wrongly referred to as a building, thereby forgetting that they are the church.[350]

Therefore, God desires that a church based upon accountability through the body would grow, where each would care for one another. Most of the early church members were being persecuted, and the edification of the church and bearing one another's burdens was the goal of each member.[351] The early church lived in a hostile environment where they were persecuted, fleeing from family, friends, and the civil authorities. They were each there to help one another and were not critical of each other in the sense that each felt subservient to the other. They displayed God's love toward each other,

---

348. 1 Peter 4:17.
349. 1 Corinthians 5:12, 13, BBE.
350. See Acts 2.
351. Galatians 6:2; Ephesians 4:2.

helped each other, and edified each other, demonstrating how to live and walk the kingdom life. There are about sixty verses in the New Testament that tell us how to help one another, encourage one another, hold each other accountable, and speak the truth in love to one another. In the early church, every person knew each other and they were involved in each other's lives. It was a very intimate circle. Many churches today are too large to know one another this intimately. Therefore, if there needs to be discipline in the church, it all presupposes that each person is living in community with each other. Unfortunately, most people in churches today do not live in an intimate spiritual understanding. As Matthew 18 teaches, we go to them individually; if they don't respond, then we go to the elders of the church; if they still don't respond, then the issue is brought before the whole church. If they still don't repent, then you treat them as non-believers (souls to be ministered to) because that is how they chose to live.

The church is the faithful bride that is marching in the direction of the kingdom. It is a community of people who bring about reconciliation, and if others in the church refuse that, then that is their choice. Only those who are known by the church can make a disciplined decision in these matters. Many times, people are disciplined by members of the body that are unknown to them. Most of us do not have an accurate perception of ourselves, and because we have blind spots, it is okay and good for certain people in the church that are close to us to help assess our situation or faith, just as the early church did. Ellen White's counsels were used heavily in this sense as the early SDA church was forming. The nine volumes of Testimonies to the Church are evidence of this. As social creatures, we need other people in our lives to keep us spiritually aligned. Just knowing that others care about me spiritually is huge. These are not people who feel superior to me, but rather they also feel that they are the worst of sinners.

Our culture in America is based on individuality. From the founding of America, it has always been based on individual freedom. Everyone has the right to life, liberty, and the pursuit of happiness. It's a foundational mantra. People feel and say, "No one has the right to tell me what to do. I can do what I want and if you tell me otherwise then you are intolerant of me." Therefore, everyone else has the responsibility to tolerate each other, and tolerance becomes a supreme virtue in this country. Only those who are not tolerated in this country become intolerant toward others. An idol of individuality rises to one of absolute tolerance of others no matter what. Yes, I would rather live in America, where individualism exists, than a country where there is a dictatorship or fascism exists, but the ideology of individualism in America is not necessarily the best for Christians. Moral relativism in the United States and perhaps other parts of the world has reached the point of "everyone do[ing] what is right in their own eyes."[352]

The value of individuality is antithetical to the kingdom and is more unlike Christ than like Christ. The kingdom life begins, not when I pursue my rights to live as I want, but when I die to my rights. I submit my rights to God, not pursuing what I think is always best for me, but rather displaying God's character in what is best for God and others. It's a high standard and not for the weak of heart, but it is the kingdom, God's character of love, being put on display. It doesn't happen overnight, but with "Not my will, but thy will be done" is the motto of a true Christian, when God lives in us, we will live for God and begin to live for others. It becomes the true motive for self-denial. Entering the body of Christ is entering a covenant with God, which is the new covenant that works by love, furthering the kingdom. The kingdom of God is distinct and countercultural. The extent to which I enter it is the extent to which I live it and put God on display. Look for opportunities to manifest the kingdom by withholding judgments of people. Ascribing worth to all and helping others grow and develop is where our spiritual discernment can be used for God's greater glory.

> *The kingdom life begins, not when I pursue my rights to live as I want, but when I die to my rights.*

Thought Questions on the Discerning Kingdom

1) How can we ascribe an unsurpassable and unconditional worth to all the people we meet?

2) What is the defining characteristic of "being children of our Father in heaven" (Matthew 5)? How does it affect your life?

3) How do we stifle the judgment of others?

4) How does judgment block the flow of God's love?

5) What is the difference between good judgment and evil judgment?

6) What keeps us in balance so that we avoid judging others?

7) How can a culture of individuality be destructive?

---

352. Judges 17:6.

Kingdom Unity

We have seen how the kingdom is unique and grows dynamically. However, this chapter focuses on the key to the whole concept of the kingdom. God's desire has always been to recreate Himself in us and dwell within us, joining us in an intimate relationship. It has been hidden from the ages, but now has been revealed, as Paul stated in Colossians 1:26-27. "Christ in you is the hope of glory" is the key to what the kingdom is all about. The degree to shich we live this is the degree to which we are in union with Christ. Paul says that this is the mystery that has been hidden from the ages, which is the hope of glory, but in verse 27 he states that the *"glorious riches"* are revealed within the mystery. Therefore, not only is the hope of glory revealed when Christ is in you but also the glorious riches of Christ are revealed when He is present within you, especially in relation to the gentiles, those not knowing Christ. What is unique in this passage is that God desired this and it has been "hid from the ages." God had always wanted to reveal Himself in us "ages and ages" ago, however Satan had a controversy over Christ having the power to recreate mankind in the image of God.

Furthermore, ever since the fall of man, the controversy has continued in that Satan has always been trying to block mankind from a relationship with God. Christ's death and resurrection broke down the wall of separation for the reality of 'Christ in you the hope of glory' to take place.

Jesus had purchased us back from Satan for this to become a reality. He also made us ambassadors for Him so that the reality can become known to others. He has distinctly stated that we can share in His life experience and love of the Father throughout eternity. As previously mentioned, it is the *perecherosis* that God has given to us so that we can mutually dwell within one another. Dwelling within one another upon the foundation of self-sacrificial love for one another is what God desires for us, and throughout eternity we can participate in that reality.

Jesus has given us the ability to participate in the "fullness of God"[353] to reveal "the riches of his glory (character)."[354] It's a beautiful thought to realize that Jesus has opened to us the same experience that He has with the Father and we can receive His fullness. As stated earlier, Jesus prays "that they may be one just as we are one." God's love is revealed in and through us as we participate in God's divine nature. Peter states that through His promises we can "participate in the divine nature."[355] There can be nothing more awesome and beautiful than God's desire to share His divine nature in and through us. Also, there is nothing better God could offer us than participating in His divine nature and experiencing the agape, unconditional, and unsurpassable love that the Godhead shares with each other. One thing must be noted—we never become God; that would be pantheism. In addition, it's not possible because otherwise, love would not be the ultimate reality. [356] The fact is you need two personal, moral agents who reciprocate love. If we were fused into God, there would be no relationship. Anyone who believes they become god are just buying into Satan's lies and the non-reality of this fact. We don't become Christ, but rather we become one with Christ. We are forever distinct from God. However, we can enjoy the love relationship that God desires for us.

The same love the Father has towards the Son, He has towards us because we are in the Son. Every second we live in God, God is living in us. Being aware of His presence in us, through faith, is the key to being fully awake, reciprocating love, and ascribing worth toward others. Also, since Christ is in us, the hope of revealing His character is for His glory, and the extent to which we surrender to God is the degree to which this becomes true. A daily dying and surrendering by faith each moment in Christ are the source of this revelation. Many of us don't experience it

---

353. Ephesians 3:19.
354. Colossians 1:27.
355. 2 Peter 1:4, ISV.
356. 1 John 4:8.

and see it because our minds have become dull and indolent toward the reality of that truth. Our fallen environment draws us into a zombielike stupor and we become blinded by the powers of this world. However, it is true that we are recipients of an unlimited and undefinable love, and as, we grow and experience the capacity of Christ dwelling within us, we put on display God's character of love to the world. We need to affirm that it is true and believe it is true no matter what we feel or experience in any given second of our lives or whether we're having a good day or bad day. The fact that we are loved with the same love that the eternal Godhead share with each other and have since all eternity is amazing.

When we are in union with Christ, we may suffer with Christ, but we share with God's glory. Paul describes this: "The Spirit bears witness with our spirit that we are the children of God and if children, then heirs; heirs of God, and joint heirs with Christ, in fact, that we share in his sufferings in order that we may share in his glory."[357] Becoming an heir with Christ is inheriting the right of Sonship with Christ. Therefore, the kingdom is revealed when we see a self-sacrificial lifestyle that reflects Calvary love. As we became joint heirs with Christ, we are joint heirs in His sufferings as well. The Greek word for "suffer" is *sumpascho* (sym—together, pascho—passion), which birthed the English word "sympathy." Therefore, Jesus shares with our suffering. Greg Boyd says, "As we learn to yield to Christ within us and he increasingly forms his character in us, we find ourselves in conflict with the ways of the world, as Christ was. And this is the cause of the distinctive kind of suffering that the New Testament means by 'suffering with Christ.'[358] A good illustration of this is when there are conjoined twins. Sometimes one twin will feel the pain or laughter of the other. When we suffer, God is participating in our suffering. Hebrews says, "For we do not have a high priest incapable of sympathizing with our weakness, but one who has been tempted in every way just as we are, yet without

> *Jesus could sympathize with us because even though He didn't sin, He experienced life from our perspective. He too knew the struggles of the flesh and the temptations that fell upon Him. As a matter of fact, His struggle against sin was much greater than ours would ever be.*

---

357. Romans 8:16, 17, ISV.
358. Greg Boyd, Benefit of the Doubt (Grand Rapids, MI: Baker Books, 2013) 246.

sin."[359] Jesus can sympathize with us because even though He didn't sin, He experienced life from our perspective. He also knew the struggles of the flesh and the temptations that fell upon Him. As a matter of fact, His struggle against sin was much greater than ours would ever be. Christ alone accomplished the atonement on behalf of all mankind, so we replicate the cross experience in this world by participating in His sufferings for His name's sake. Furthermore, God suffers with us. Paul Fiddes points out that, "if the cross of Jesus tells us that God is in pain then God's power can hardly be that of the human absolute monarch who shows his supremacy by avoiding pain; it could only be a power of a love that is made perfect in weakness. Sufferers rightly protest against their suffering. God protests with the protesters because God also suffers. There is a mutuality between the two experiences: if God suffers then God also protests, and a God who protests against suffering cannot be the cause of it, or God would be protesting against Himself."[360]

Even our persecution is related to Christ. The fact is that Satan attacks us because Christ is in us. Our suffering is not about us, but about Christ. Satan desires to destroy Christ in us by destroying us. He also desires to destroy the glorification of Christ through us, thereby attempting to vindicate his accusations against God in the great controversy. However, only true love can be obedient. When our union is with Christ, agape love becomes an ontological experience that we can only have when Christ is in us and we in Him. Otherwise, how can we love our enemies? It's humanly impossible to love our enemies, and therefore it states in Hebrews 5:8 "he learned (the) obedience (of love) through sufferings." Becoming obedient to His Father inevitably led Him to suffering and even death. The Greek word for "obedience" is *hupakoe*, which is from the root *hupo*, meaning "under." Jesus came under his Father rather than over Him. He was tempted in the garden to forsake His will, which would have been an *"over"* rather than *"under"* experience, but he came 'under' and did not rebel against his Father's will and desire. Jesus put His submission 'under' the Father's will.

Paul felt so deeply connected with Christ that he felt that his beatings were Christ's beatings. He states this in several epistles.[361] Jesus also connected His sufferings to His church. In Acts, Jesus said to Saul, "Saul, Saul, why are you attacking me so cruelly? And he said, who are you,

---

359. Hebrews 4:15, NET.
360. Paul Fiddes, Participating in God (Louisville, KY: Westminster John Knox Press, 2000) 161, 162.
361. 2 Corinthians 1:5; Colossians 1:24; 1 Peter 4:13.

Lord? And he said, I am Jesus, whom you are attacking."[362] Jesus identified Himself with His church body on an incarnational level. As Saul persecuted the church, Jesus was truly sympathizing and identifying with His people to the extent that whoever hurt them hurt Him. Zechariah 2:8 puts it this way: *"for anyone who touches you, touches the pupil of his eye."* Jesus is so connected to His people that whoever hurts them hurts Him in the most excruciating way. As we share abundantly in Christ's sufferings, we will also share in His glory. Paul realized that it was his privilege to participate in Christ's sufferings, even rejoicing in his sufferings for Christ's sake.[363]

We are united with Christ even in sufferings, and that is the beauty of experiencing and even displaying God's love. Realize that with any suffering we experience, Christ is on the inside of our suffering. When we suffer or sacrifice for the kingdom, we can rejoice in it. While certain sufferings come from the wars that are upon this earth, our spiritual warfare is not earthly, but based upon principalities and powers in wicked and high, spiritual places.

Therefore, seeking first the kingdom is seeking first to dwell in God, and when that happens, He enters into His people. The sanctuary service displayed that man was participating in the death and life of the Son. Mankind could now rejoice, because as he became a spiritual priest, he could enter the holy place and partake of Christ's life in the bread (the Word), the oil (the Spirit), and the incense (the prayers) of God himself.

Also, when we rejoice in Christ's suffering, we also participate in Christ's joy. His joy is our joy. Hebrews 12:2 states that for the "joy that was set before him, he endured the cross, despised the shame and sat down on the right hand of God." Even though Jesus despised the shame of the cross, He chose to focus on the joy of what the cross would accomplish. Jesus envisioned what His suffering would accomplish through anticipating how His work on the cross would break down barriers[364] and free people from all oppression and sin. Jesus was glorifying His Father by displaying His love for all mankind, and because only love can break down the barriers that sin set up, only love can transform us. Therefore, when we surrender our lives to Christ, we also participate in His same joy. Jesus said in John 17:13, *"And now I am coming to you, and I say these things in the world so that they may have my joy made complete in themselves."* Though the cross

---

362. Acts 9:4, 5, BBE.
363. 2 Corinthians 4:10-18.
364. Ephesians 2:14-16.

was before Jesus, He had this joy and desired that this same joy would now be manifested in all of His disciples. Jesus said He wanted His joy in them. He wanted the full measure within them so that they could share in His joy and further the purposes of the Father's will in this world. Therefore, amid suffering, Jesus wanted His joy in us so that we can envision, as He did, what the sufferings will do for God's glory.

Every self-sacrificial thing we do and every Spirit-led servant act we commit in Christ has profound effects that display God's love to others and the universe. Paul reiterates that those who follow Christ become a "spectacle" before the world and angels, displaying the character of God.[365] The greater joy is to realize that God uses us to put Him on display throughout eternity. What a legacy to leave behind, to be used of God in such a way! The glory of the kingdom is allowing God to use you in a way that reveals His unconditional and unsurpassable agape love that will be displayed throughout eternity. The beauty of the cross was that Jesus was crucified by His enemies, whom He loved and for whom He died, especially considering He had the omnipotent power to destroy them. Love is defined as Jesus on the cross dying for all humanity. God's glory of the kingdom is to give Himself away so that people have faith in the power of His love.[366] That is also the glory of the Godhead, where each One gives Himself to the other and comes under the other. It's a self-sacrificial circle of love, and when we participate in the love of God, it motivates us to participate in His sufferings, which then allows us to experience a different facet of the glory and joy of Christ.

Our role is to surrender to this love, and even that is a gift.[367] To the degree that we do surrender, God's love motivates us to divest ourselves of self and sacrifice whatever is needed. Living in the glory of the kingdom is becoming more aware and appreciative of what God has done in Jesus Christ. If we allow God, He will provide the power to disengage our worldly patterns and transform us, fashion us, and mold us to reflect His image. When we allow God to be recreated in our minds, minds shaped by the fallen world will be cast out.

So many times, the clouds of this life block out the sun. Many know that the geographical areas of the United States have cloud coverage many days of the year, just as England is prone to have. Many of us realize that when we fly on a plane and above the clouds, we see the beautiful sun in

---

365. 1 Corinthians 4:9.
366. John 3:16; 1 John 3:16.
367. Romans 2:4.

all its glory. The Son is always there, but life's obstacles are like the clouds that obscure our ability to see the Son. Yes, we cause some of these issues ourselves, and we would be surprised to know that probably most of them are products of our bad decisions. However, even the situations that come upon us in unexpected ways, like a curve ball, triggers our human nature to focus on the clouds, and the degree in which I live under them is the degree to which my problems will seem monumental. This concept is like what Solomon spoke of in Ecclesiastes— "under the sun" was a metaphor for worldly thinking.

We typically change our picture of God based on our feelings, emotions, or experiences, but God never changes,[368] and there are no inconsistencies or shifting shadows[369] in who He is, but our experiences in Christ usually fluctuate. The questions are: How do we live in the light of the Son, rather than under the clouds? How do we get our hearts and minds to align with the truth in Christ? Behold Him and He will change you. We start with focusing on and appreciating the crucified Son, thereby allowing us to be more capable of entering fellowship with Him.

Jesus said, "if I am lifted up I will draw all men unto myself." The word "men" is supplied; therefore, when we lift up (huposoo = elevate) Jesus, then He will "draw" (helkuo = compel) all to Him. This describes the power of His love to compel[370] and that His whole government and universe is based on His love. James Thompson states, "Those who identify with the crucified Christ seek the good of the other rather than their self-fulfillment. To have the mind of Christ (Phil. 2:5) is to humble oneself for others. Love extends not only to those of one social class or ethnic group but to all for whom Christ died. Those who are 'not conformed to this world' do not retreat from it, but offer an example of new humanity that has torn down barriers between peoples, demonstrated love for the weak and provided a common mindset based upon a shared story."[371] Only those who are not conformed, but rather transformed, are capable of offering this example of love. God desires to draw us into a mutual love covenant relationship with Him. He desires to dwell within His people[372] so that they can participate in the same love the Son shares with the

---

368. Hebrews 13:8.
369. James 1:17, ISV.
370. "The term figuratively expresses the supernatural power of the love of God which goes out to all." Theological Dictionary of the New Testament, abridged, Bromiley, p. 227.
371. James Thompson, *Moral Formation According to Paul* (Grand rapids, MI: Baker Academics, 2013), 212-213.
372. Exodus 25:8; John 14:7; 17:23; Luke 17:21; Colossians 1:27; Revelation 21:3; Phil. 2:5.

Father.[373] No matter how thick the clouds are or how many days we spend under them, we can make the daily, conscious choice to live in the fellowship of the Son. The degree to which we make this daily choice to allow God to come into our lives and fill us with His incomprehensible love, thereby changing our moment-by-moment experiences, is the degree to which we will have a kingdom experience. Therefore, live above the clouds in the radiance of the Son.

Thought Questions on Kingdom Unity

1) What was the mystery that was hidden from the ages but now revealed?

2) When mutual indwelling takes place, in what do we participate?

3) How is the kingdom revealed in your life?

4) When we are mutually indwelling with God, what else do we share with Him and why?

5) How can we break free from the clouds in our lives?

6) What should we do when we don't "feel" connected to Christ?

7) What do I need to do every day to be mutually indwelling with Christ?

---

373. John 17:23.

Maturing into the Kingdom

We previously looked at Colossians 1:27 where the mystery that was hidden from the ages has now been revealed—Christ in you, the hope of glory. The beauty of that mystery is beyond knowledge and words, but not beyond what God wants us to experience. Let's look at what verses 28 and 29 add to that message. It states, "We proclaim him (Christ in you) by instructing and teaching every man in all wisdom, so that we may present every man mature in Christ. Towards this goal I also labor, struggling according to his power that powerfully works in me."[374] First, let's look at the word "mature" (KJV— "perfect"). The Greek word used for "mature" is *teleios*, which denotes "complete." Therefore, let us repeat and enlarge what Paul presented in these verses to behold a larger picture of God's purpose. When we look at these three verses together, what Paul is saying is that the mystery of God, which is Christ in you, Paul proclaims through teaching in all wisdom *so that* every man is presented complete and mature in Christ. Paul said in Verse 29 that he struggled (*agonizomai*), 'agonizing' and 'fervently striving,' with God's energy within him to become mature. Paul was striving, along with the Colossians, to bring maturity and completeness into Christians through having the fullness of Christ in them

---

374. New English Translation.

(verse 27). Therefore, the maturing of a Christian is having the fullness of Christ in you, despite our human struggles. Also, Paul states that when Christ is in us we receive God's wisdom. Furthermore, the beginning of a reverent fear for God marks the start of wisdom.[375] James even says that if we lack wisdom God not only desires to give it to us if we ask, but He doesn't find fault with us when we ask! How freeing it is to know that God doesn't point a finger at us when we may have messed up once again but finally come to Him asking for wisdom.[376]

Paul also makes sure that the Colossians realize that it is God's power/energy that "works" in them. The Greek word for "work" is *energeio*, which we saw before. Paul is essentially saying that it is God's energy that propels us. It is the synergy of God's power and our striving that leads to spiritual completeness. Paul spoke about this in Ephesians as well. He says, "And to know the love of Christ which passeth knowledge, that ye might be filled with the fullness of God."[377] Therefore, to know and experience God's love is to know God, and to this extent, we are complete and filled with God in us. Love is defined by Jesus laying down His life for us.[378] To know love is to know this fact. There is nothing else God can give us in Christ by which we can have His full life![379] The issue is getting Christians to "mature" in Christ. It's not based on how big your church is, how much your offering is, or how elaborate your programs are, but upon wearing Christ's righteousness each day. This is the abundant life that He desires.[380]

> *It is the synergy of God's power and our striving that leads to spiritual completeness.*

One of the biggest issues that blocks our experience in Christ is the fact that we like to be entertained. We live in a very hedonistic culture where more churches and Christians desire to be entertained and find more stimulants. You can't mature in Christ if you are always looking to be entertained. When the culture invades the church, then the church tries to use the latest and greatest modes of entertainment to present programs to their members. How do we then mature? Paul said, "For though I am absent from you in body, yet I am with you in Spirit, rejoicing and seeing your order, and the firmness of your faith. Therefore, just as you received

---

375. Proverbs 9:10.
376. James 1:5; James 1:2-4.
377. Ephesians 3:19.
378. 1 John 3:16.
379. 1 John 3:16; Ephesians 3:19.
380. John 10:10.

Christ Jesus as Lord, continue to live your lives in him, rooted and built up in him and firm in your faith just as you were taught, and overflowing with thankfulness."[381] Paul delights in the discipline of the Colossians. We can see that growth is always contingent on being disciplined and carrying out God's directives. Paul is also encouraged to see how firm they are in the faith, both in prayer and through the Word. Therefore, because they are disciplined, they are solid.

Paul says to the Colossians to keep on that track. He says in verse 6, "just as you received Christ as Lord continue to live your life in him." The word "continue" in Greek is *paripateo*. It means to walk in a certain way or to walk around. Paul uses other terms as it relates to "continue," such as walking in the Spirit,[382] walk worthy of the Lord,[383] and walk as children of light.[384] Paul emphasizes the importance of not only receiving the Lord but also continuing to walk in a way that reflects God's Lordship in you and being disciplined in it. The verb "walk" (*peripateo*) is in the present, active, imperative voice. In other words, it's always present and active. We are carrying out an imperative command and continue to walk in that command. In each present moment, the command will never be past tense. The theme is similar in 2 Timothy 2:3-4. Paul commends the Colossians for continuing to walk in this *peripateo*, present, imperative command. After that, Paul says to be "rooted and established in the faith." The Greek word for root is *rhizoo*, which is the root of a tree. Therefore, Paul is telling them to be established and rooted like a tree in the way they walk, like what Isaiah says in 61:3: "that they may be called trees of righteousness the planting of the Lord, that he may be glorified." The metaphor is that we walk in such a way that a tree is rooted. Every step we take is like getting deeper roots, and we become more established in righteousness in order to glorify God. Like a tree, the roots grow stronger with nourishment from being in Christ, and as they become stronger, the tree grows taller. Therefore, the roots of this tree are Christ, like John 15 and the parable of the vine. The branches are connected to the vine, which is rooted in the ground. The degree to which we walk this way is the degree to which we have Christ rooted deeper in us. We get our life from Christ, our values from Christ, our identity from Christ, and our worth from Christ. Each of our steps is rooted in Christ through this moment-by-moment, step-by-step experience.

---

381. Colossians 2:5-7, NET.
382. Galatians 5:16.
383. 1 Thessalonians 2:12.
384. Ephesians 5:8.

The problem that blocks this experience for us is that we in America (and other parts of the world) compartmentalize our lives between the holy and the secular. We are usually in a holy mode when we are at church, when we pray, or when Christ is on our mind, but a lot of times our minds are on the ordinary and mundane world. When our minds are common or secular, then we are not awake to the Spirit and Christ is not in our minds. Our walks are just like those of other commoners of the world. Our minds become totally consumed by the secular world around us, and we become defined by our surroundings. We are immersed in the tasks at hand. When we are grocery shopping, our minds are there; when driving the car, we're thinking of where we are going or what we are doing next, or we may have the radio on, which further distracts us from Christ. Otherwise, the car ride would be a great time for praying or listening to something that keeps us spiritually aligned in Christ. Unfortunately, most of the time, our minds push Christ out, and we're not even aware of it. Paul exhorts his readers to have Christ in them, not just some of the time, but every moment. The extent to which Christ is out of our minds is the degree to which we have a secular mind. Not only that, but it's easy for our minds to redefine who God is when we don't have Him in our minds. We allow the world to squeeze us into its mold.[385] Remember that when we surrender our lives, the life we surrender is the life that we live on a moment-by-moment basis. Therefore, the surrendered life of Christ is the present life that we surrender every moment. This surrender is a real and actual surrender of mind and body. It is not an abstract surrender, like professing to do something but not taking the initiative to deliver on our profession. The mind of Christ is dynamic, active, and real; it's not a mental ascent to truth, but rather an experiential life that is lived.

The goal is to tear down the differences between holy and common, sacred and secular. When we allow God to dwell within us, we invite the kingdom to live in us every second. That is what Jesus meant when He said to bring the kingdom to earth. Every moment is to be under the dome; the King is to reign in our lives. That is the kingdom. Again let us not confuse knowing about the kingdom with knowing and experiencing the kingdom. Remember, the kingdom is Jesus, when transformed by Jesus, we are living the kingdom. Paul challenges us to walk surrendered as the Colossians did every moment. When our lives are planted by Christ, then and only then do we grow and become firmly established and rooted in Christ. When we integrate the kingdom into everyday life, the division

---

385. Romans 12:2.

between common and holy disappears and all becomes holy as we walk in that holiness of life.

Paul told the Corinthians to check whether they are in the faith. That recommendation is for us as well. He doesn't necessarily mean to take inventory of our lives, even though there's nothing wrong with that occasionally, but rather to make sure we are in the faith moment-by-moment. We can realize that whatever we do during the day, God is in us doing it through us to perform His purposes and desires. Ellen White states that when we do this consistently, we won't even be aware that we are doing it. She says, "If the human agent consents, God can and will so identify His will with all our thoughts and aims, so blend our hearts and minds into conformity to his Word, that when obeying his will, we are only carrying out the impulses of our own minds. All such will not possess an unsanctified, selfish disposition, ready to carry out their own wills, but will have a jealous, earnest, determined zeal for the glory (character) of God." [386] When we are aware of it, we will live this promise: "Through him then let us offer up a sacrifice continually, that is the fruit of our lips that confess his name."[387]

Living the *peripateo* life is living the life that is present and active for God. It creates a jealousy for God and glory of His name. It brings to fruition in the believer that the highest honor is to live and, if necessary, die for the glory of God.

Thought Questions on Maturing into the Kingdom

1) According to this chapter, what predetermines my maturity in Christ?

2) What is the metaphor that Paul and Jesus use for being solidly grounded in the faith?

3) How can I walk in the peripateo way?

4) How does my view of God change when I walk in a 'rooted' walk?

5) How can we distinguish between the "common" and the "holy"?

6) What happens when we integrate the kingdom life into our everyday lives?

---

386. Ellen White, *Bible Echo.* July 20, 1896.
387. Hebrews 13:15, NHEB.

Kingdom Indwelled Transformation

The culmination of the Kingdom Transformation happens when Christ the Bride-groom receives His bride, [388] a completed people in the form of the church, Christ's bride. Knowing about God is easier than knowing God. Some can become pastors, get theology degrees, and even know the bible pretty well, but it doesn't equate to knowing God. The story of the ten virgins in Matthew 25 contrasts 5 who were ready and 5 who were not ready. They all were sleeping, and only when they heard that the bride-groom was coming did they then prepare themselves.

The foolish virgins knew about God but the wise virgins knew God. They perhaps shared the same beliefs, church pews, and both were pure, good morale people. However, those that knew about God were rejected at the door. They believed they should have gone in;[389] they lived good moral lives, wasn't that enough! Jesus says depart from me I never *knew* you. The word "know" in Greek is *Ginosko,* it not only is a very intimate word but it deals with an experiential knowledge, not just a mental assent to truth or head knowledge. It is an intimate experience that takes place between two people. Even though the foolish virgins trimmed their lamps, to make them brighter, it was too late they ran out of oil. Jesus is saying to the 5 foolish virgins, I never knew you, we were never intimate. They didn't prioritize their relationship with God. It should have been deeper and more intimate. However, there was never a deeper experience; it was only surface at best. Jesus said in Mt. 12:50 that, *"whoever shall do the*

---
388. Rev. 19:7
389. See also Mt. 7:21-23

will of the Father the same is my brother, and my sister and my mother." The word for will is *thelema* in Greek. It can be translated as "inclination." Therefore, doing God's will, means that his will is implanted in you. God's inclinations and desires will run through you because Christ is in you. When Jesus looks at his children he will see a reflection of Himself. Regarding the foolish virgins, Jesus rejected them, because they were not one or united with Him on a personal level. And when his believers are one with Him they become one with each other.

John 17 verse 22 and verse 23 describe this oneness. Remember Jesus is speaking to His father. Verse 22 reads, *"the glory (doxa – character) which **thou** (the Father) gave **me** (Jesus) I have given **them** (believers); that **they** (the believers) may be one, even as **we** are one."* Let this truth sink in.

It is God in me that is capable of being one with God in you. This is true unity. It isn't me getting to know you better. It is God in me that Communicates with God in you. This is the foundation of oneness. In addition, we can see how that the Godhead shares this mutual indwelling within each other.

Verse 23 reads, *"I (Jesus) in **them** (believers), and **thou** (the Father) in **me** (Jesus) that (or "in order that) **they** (believers) may be **perfect** (teleioo – completed) in one; and that the world may **know** (Ginosko – intimate experiential knowledge) that **thou** (the Father) sent **me** (Jesus) and **thou** (the Father) has loved **them** (believers) as thou has loved **me** (Jesus)."* Therefore, the only way that the world will be convicted of God's love and of Jesus is when we give God the privilege of indwelling Himself in us through the Spirit.

This dwelling is found in both the Old and New Testaments. In Exodus 25:8 it states, *"Let them make me a sanctuary that I might dwell with them."* Some Hebrew scholars use the words *"dwell in them."* The whole sanctuary message ended with an indwelling experience with God. That is why Paul says that we are a temple bought with a price.[390] When all individual temples (believers) are united and one with God we will see emerging a big Jesus on earth. Only then will the mind of Christ be connected with His body, the church. This body experience is perfectly described by Paul in 1 Cor. 12.

In correlation to the quote we saw in the Old Testament about God dwelling with His people, we also see that Jesus commented this in John 14:2 and verse 3. *"In my Father's house are many mansions (mone -dwelling places); if it were not so I would have told you. I go to prepare a place for you. And if I go to prepare a place for you, I will come again, and receive you unto*

---

390. 1 Cor. 6:19; 1 Cor. 3:16

myself; that where I am, there ye may be also." The King James Version has the word "mansions," however the Greek word *mone* of which the root is *meno* means abide or dwell. We see Jesus stating that in my Fathers house there are many dwelling or abiding places, a direct reference to the sanctuary. This is also spoken of within the Jewish marriage context. In ancient Jewish weddings the betrothal marked a ceremony followed by a feast which officially inaugurated the couple into the new betrothal covenant. This would be related to the last supper where Christ offered the *Mohar* (dowry= His death) for the bride price and would go back to His Father's house to prepare a room for His bride. This is found in John 14; 2 and 3.

"In my Father 's house are many mansions (dwelling rooms); if it were not so I would have told you, I go to prepare a place for you, And if I go and prepare a place for you, I will come again, and receive you unto myself; that where I am, there ye may be also." God has always desired an abiding experience such as this. Jesus even stated, *"But he that shall endure to the end, the same shall be saved."* Many people equate enduring with "hanging in there," or using extra strength to make it. However the Greek word *hupomeno* is defined as "abiding under," *hupo* is under and *meno* is abide. Therefore, Jesus says those who will be saved are those who abide in me or abide under me. What's interesting is that the previous verse, verse 12, contrasts this experience. It mentions, *"...and because of iniquity (lawlessness) will increase the love of many shall wax (or grow) cold."* The word "cold" in Greek is *psucho* where we get the English word *pyscho* from. Therefore, what it truly states is that those who reject the "abiding under" experience become a "lawless" one. When we reject the love towards God, our natures wax cold against God's mercy, grace and love. We become desensitized thereby becoming psucho or pyscho, out of a stable mind and into an unstable mind. As Philippians 2:5 states putting on Christ's mind keeps us stable and humble, thereby emptying ourselves of self and replacing our minds with Christ. But as Romans 1:24-28 states, when God gives us over to a reprobate mind we become morally empty. So the giving up, or rejecting of the "abiding under," experience creates a mental illness which appears to be a self-absorption of darkness, or emptiness. Therefore, abiding in Christ creates the antithesis which is having God's mind in us and the life of Christ becomes glorified through us.

Jesus says, *"Do you not believe that I am in the Father and the Father is in me? The words that I say to you I do not speak on my own initiative, but the Father abiding in me does His works."* This verse describes that it is the abiding of the Father in Christ that does the works! Jesus isn't taking credit for his works he states that it is the Father that works through Him. As Christ works through us it is Christ that does the works in us as well. We can't take credit for anything that glorifies Christ. But Jesus further states in verse 13 *"whatever you ask in my name, that will I do, that (in order that) the Father may be glorified in the Son."* Here we can see that the Father gets the glory through the Son in us. Therefore, the Father gets the glory through us! What a beautiful thought.

Our only priority is to accept Jesus' death as ours and receive His life. When we receive His life through a moment-by-moment experience, Jesus can then blend our thoughts with his and in the end we will be carrying out His desires thereby giving glory to the Father.

If you have questions or would like to schedule a speaking engagement, please email me:

Kevin Michalek
http://1ref.us/hh

Bibliography

Andreason, M.L. *The Sanctuary Service.* Hagerstown, MD: Review & Herald, 1947.

Billings, J. Todd. *Union with Christ.* Grand Rapids, MI: Baker Books, 2011.

Bonaparte, Napoleon. *Napoleon's argument for the divinity of Christ and the Scriptures: in a conversation with General Bertrand, at St. Helena.* Charleston, SC: South Carolina Tract Society, 1861.

Bonhoeffer, Dietrich. *The Cost of Discipleship.* New York: Simon and Schuster Publishing, 1995.

Bonhoeffer, Dietrich. *Ethics.* New York: Simon and Schuster Publishing, 1995.

Boyd, Gregory. *Benefit of the Doubt.* Grand Rapids, MI: Baker Books, 2013.

Boyd, Gregory. *Myth of a Christian Nation.* Grand Rapids, MI: Zondervan, 2005.

Christopherson, Jeff. *Kingdom Matrix.* Boise, ID: Russel Media, 2012.

Crook, J.A. *Law and Roman Life of Rome 90 BC – 212 AD.* Ithica, NY: Cornell University, 1984.

Edershiem, Alfred. *The Temple*. Grand Rapids, MI: E.B. Eerdmans, 1990.

Fiddes, Paul. *Participating in God*. Louisville, KY: Westminster John Knox Press, 2000.

Freud, Sigmund, *Theories and Concepts*. AROPA, 2013.

Gifford, James D. *Perichoretic Salvation*. Eugene, OR: WIPF Stock Press, 2011.

Jennings, Timothy. *The God-Shaped Brain*. Downers Grove, IL: Intervarsity Press, 2013.

Kittel, Gerhard, and Gerhard Friedrich. *Theological Dictionary of the New Testament*.

Translated by Geoffrey W. Bromily. Grand Rapids, MI: W.B. Eerdmans, 1986.

Lewis, C.S., *Mere Christianity*. New York: The Macmillan Co., 1972.

Onions, C.T. ed. *The Oxford Dictionary of English Etymology*. Oxford: Oxford University Press, 1966.

Robertson, O. Palmer. *The Christ of the Covenants*. Phillisburg: P & R Pub., 1980.

Schaeffer, Francis. *The God Who is There*. Downers Grove, Il: Intervarsity Press, 1968.

Stott, John W. *The Cross of Christ*. Downers Grove, Il: Intervarsity Press, 1986.

Thompson, James. *Moral Formation According to Paul*. Grand Rapids, MI: Baker Academic, 2013

Tonstad, Sigve K. *Savings God's Reputation*. New York: T & T Clark, 2006.

Trumbull, H. Clay. *Blood Covenant*, Quoted in James D. Gifford Jr. *Perichoretic Salvation*. Eugene: WIPF and Stock, 2011.

Van Noye, Albert. *Old Testament Priests and the New Priest*. Petersham: Mass. St. Bedes Pub., 1980.

Van Gemeren, William A. ed. *New International Dictionary and Old Testament Theology & Exegesis*. Grand Rapids, MI: Zondervan Pub., 1997.

White, Ellen G. "Bible Echo", July 20, 1896.

White, Ellen G. *Confrontation*. Washington, DC: Review & Herald Publishing Association, 1971.

White, Ellen G. *Early Writings*. Washington, DC: Review and Herald Publishing Association, 1882.

White, Ellen G. *The Great Controversy*. Mountain View, CA: Pacific Press Publishing Association, 1911.

White, Ellen G. "The Kingdom of Christ", *Advent and Sabbath Review and Herald*, Vol. 73, no. 33, August 18, 1896.

White, Ellen G. *Patriarchs and Prophets*. Washington, DC: Review and Herald Publishing Association, 1890.

Yoder, John. *The Politics of Jesus*. Grand Rapids, MI: W.B. Eerdmans, 1983.

TEACH Services, Inc.
PUBLISHING

We invite you to view the complete
selection of titles we publish at:
www.TEACHServices.com

We encourage you to write us
with your thoughts about this,
or any other book we publish at:
info@TEACHServices.com

TEACH Services' titles may be purchased in
bulk quantities for educational, fund-raising,
business, or promotional use.
bulksales@TEACHServices.com

Finally, if you are interested in seeing
your own book in print, please contact us at:
publishing@TEACHServices.com

We are happy to review your manuscript at no charge.

www.ingramcontent.com/pod-product-compliance
Lightning Source LLC
Chambersburg PA
CBHW050554160426
43199CB00015B/2652